The ESSENT

D0454061

FRENCH

Miriam Ellis, Ph.D.
University of California
Santa Cruz, California

Research and Education Association
61 Ethel Road West
Piscataway, New Jersey 08854

THE ESSENTIALS®
OF FRENCH

1997 PRINTING

Printed in the United States of America

Library of Congress Catalog Card Number 94-65504

International Standard Book Number 0-87891-926-0

WHAT "THE ESSENTIALS" WILL DO FOR YOU

This book is a review and study guide. It is comprehensive and it is concise.

It helps in preparing for exams, in doing homework, and remains a handy reference source at all times.

It condenses the vast amount of detail characteristic of the subject matter and summarizes the essentials of the field.

It will thus save hours of study and preparation time.

The book provides quick access to the important principles, vocabulary, grammar, and structures in the language.

Materials needed for exams can be reviewed in summary form – eliminating the need to read and re-read many pages of textbook and class notes. The summaries will even tend to bring detail to mind that had been previously read or noted.

This "ESSENTIALS" book has been prepared by an expert in the field, and has been carefully reviewed to assure accuracy and maximum usefulness.

Dr. Max Fogiel
Program Director

Contents

Chapter 1
THE SOUNDS OF FRENCH 1
  1.1   Pronunciation Hints 1
  1.2   The International Phonetic Alphabet (IPA) 2
  1.3   The French Alphabet 5
  1.4   Accents 6
  1.5   Liaison 7
  1.6   Elision 7
  1.7   Syllabification 8

Chapter 2
COGNATES — WORDS YOU RECOGNIZE 9
  2.1   Cognates Common to Both Languages 9
  2.2   Cognates with Minor Spelling Changes 9
  2.3   Spelling Pitfalls 10
  2.4   *"Faux amis"* (False Friends) 10
  2.5   Some Borrowed Words 11
  2.6   Capitalization 11

Chapter 3
BY THE NUMBERS 13
  3.1   Counting from 1 to 1,000,000,000 13
  3.2   Telling Time 15
  3.3   Describing Time 16
  3.4   Days of the Week 16
  3.5   Months 17
  3.6   The Four Seasons: *Les quatre saisons* 17
  3.7   Expressing the Year 17
  3.8   Phone Numbers 18
  3.9   Expressing Age 18
  3.10 Calculations 18
  3.11 Comparisons 18
  3.12 Ordinal Numbers 20

Chapter 4

NOUNS AND ARTICLES **21**

4.1   Gender 21
4.2   Formation of Feminine Nouns 25
4.3   Plural Nouns 26
4.4   The Article 28
4.5   Special Uses of the Definite Article 30
4.6   The Indefinite Article 32

Chapter 5

THE PARTITIVE ARTICLE *(Le Partitif)* **33**

5.1   General Use 33
5.2   Formation 33
5.3   Omission of the Definite Article after *"de"* 34
5.4   Definite, Indefinite, or Partitive Article 35

Chapter 6

ADJECTIVES **37**

6.1   Function 37
6.2   Formation of Feminine 37
6.3   Position of Adjectives 38
6.4   Comparing with Adjectives 41
6.5   Possessive Adjectives 44
6.6   Demonstrative Adjectives ("this," "these") 45
6.7   Interrogative Adjectives 46
6.8   Adjectives of Number 47
6.9   *Demi(e):* Half 47
6.10   Indefinite Adjectives 47

Chapter 7

PRONOUNS **49**

7.1   Subject Pronouns 49
7.2   Direct Object Pronouns 50
7.3   Indirect Object Pronouns 51
7.4   With Two Verbs Together 52
7.5   With Two Object Pronouns Together 52
7.6   *Y* and *en; penser à; parler de* 53
7.7   Interrogative Sentences with Pronouns 55
7.8   Disjunctive Pronouns 56

7.9   Relative Pronouns 56
7.10   Possessive Pronouns 58

Chapter 8
VERBS **60**
8.1   *L'indicatif* 60
8.2   *L'impératif* 64
8.3   *Le passé composé* 66
8.4   *L'imparfait* 70
8.5   *Le plus-que-parfait* 73
8.6   *Le futur proche* 74
8.7   *Le futur* 74
8.8   *Le conditionnel* 75
8.9   *L'infinitif* 77
8.10   *Le participe présent* 78
8.11   *Les verbes pronominaux* 79
8.12   Two Other Past Tenses of the Indicative 80

Chapter 9
THE SUBJUNCTIVE **82**
9.1   Formation: Regular Verbs 82
9.2   Uses of the Subjunctive in Subordinate Clauses 83
9.3   Uses of Subjunctive after Certain Conjunctions 86
9.4   *Le passé du subjonctif* 87

Chapter 10
ADVERBS **89**
10.1   Formation of Adverbs 89
10.2   Irregular Forms 90
10.3   Placement of the Adverb 90
10.4   Comparative of Adverbs 92
10.5   The Superlative 92
10.6   Some Common Adverbs 92
10.7   Interrogative Adverbs 93
10.8   Adverbs that Connect Nouns, Phrases, and Clauses .. 93

Chapter 11
PREPOSITIONS AND CONJUNCTIONS **94**
11.1   Prepositions 94

11.2	Compound Prepositions	94
11.3	Prepositions with Geographic Names	95
11.4	Common Verbs + Preposition + Infinitive	96
11.5	Conjunctions	97

Chapter 12
BASIC IDIOMATIC EXPRESSIONS **98**

12.1	Expressions with *avoir*	98
12.2	Expressions with *faire*	99
12.3	Impersonal Expressions with *il*	101
12.4	Idiomatic Expressions with *être*	103
12.5	The Verb *manquer*	103
12.6	Measuring Time with *depuis/depuis que*	104
12.7	*Connaître* and *savoir*	105
12.8	Miscellaneous Expressions	105

Chapter 13
NEGATION **107**

13.1	Positive and Negative Adverbial Expressions	107
13.2	*Quelque chose de/rien de* + Adjective	108

Chapter 14
USEFUL VOCABULARY **110**

14.1	School *(L'école)*	110
14.2	Animals *(Un animal; Les animaux)*	110
14.3	The Body *(Le corps)*	111
14.4	The City *(La ville)*	111
14.5	Clothing *(Les vêtements)*	112
14.6	Colors *(Les couleurs)*	112
14.7	Drinks *(Les boissons)*	112
14.8	The Family *(La famille)*	113
14.9	Foods *(Les aliments)*	113
14.10	Illnesses *(Les maladies)*	114
14.11	Professions, Occupations *(Les professions, les métiers)*	115

GLOSSARY **116**

CHAPTER 1

The Sounds of French

1.1 Pronunciation Hints

French is one of the Romance languages (the others are Spanish, Italian, Portuguese, Romanian, Catalan, and Provençal) and is "vocalic" in its sound, i.e., based on vowels. This structure gives the language its soft and flowing character. English speakers can attain good pronunciation if the following simple rules are kept in mind:

- There are **no diphthongs** in French, as there are in English: "boy" = "aw," "ee," "yuh." French vowels are clean and pure; e.g., *imiter* = "ee-mee-tay" (to imitate) and should be formed without any secondary movement of the jaw.
- Every syllable is of **equal importance** in volume and stress; e.g., English: de/VEL/op/ment and French: *dé/ve/lop/pe/ment*. There is a slight emphasis on the last syllable in words of two or more syllables and in a group of words: *dé/li/CIEUX; Je parle franÇAIS;* but it is not a strong stress.
- Consonants are **softened:** don't "explode" your d's, t's, b's, p's, g's, and k's and your accent will improve.
- There are **two sounds** that are generally difficult for English speakers: the "r," which can be achieved by "gargling," and the "u" (as in "tu"), which is made by puckering your lips as if to whistle, while you say "ee."

1

1.1.1 Further Pronunciation Details

French has the same alphabet as English; some letters are written but are not pronounced (e.g., most final consonants: *sans, chez, tard, livres*). Exceptions to this rule are the final "c," as in *bouc* (billy goat), "f," as in *chef* (head, chief), "l," as in *formel* (formal), and "r," as in *air*.

Also silent are "h," as in *homme, héros, théâtre*, and some combinations of letters, as in *parlent, monsieur, voudraient*.

In cognates (words that we recognize from English), spelling is often different from English, with letters added, deleted or changed, giving the word a "French" look: *classe, indépendance, appartement, université*. The International Phonetic Alphabet (IPA), utilized in most good dictionaries, will help you understand the sounds of French vowels, which remain unchanged, even in different spelling groups.

1.2 The International Phonetic Alphabet (IPA)

There are 17 consonants, 16 vowels (12 oral vowels pronounced in the mouth and 4 oral vowels placed in the nasal passage), and 3 semi-vowels/semi-consonants half-way between vowels and consonants. These sounds are expressed by phonetic symbols which are always written between [ ].

1.2.1 Oral Vowels

Phonetic Symbol	French Example	English Approx.	Remarks
1. [a]	*avec*	Ah!	Open your mouth.
2. [ɑ]	*pâle*	Ahh!	Longer than [a].
3. [e]	*été*	say	Don't add "yuh."
4. [ɛ]	*elle*	elf	More open than [e].
5. [i]	*ici*	see	Smile; don't add "yuh."
6. [o]	*mot*	Moe	Don't add "wuh."
7. [ɔ]	*porte*	up	More open than [o].
8. [ø]	*peu*	put	Lips very rounded.
9. [œ]	*soeur*	purr	More open than [ø].
10. [u]	*nous*	noose	Don't add "wuh."

2

| 11. [y] | *tu* | No English equivalent | Round your lips as if to whistle while saying "ee." |
| 12. [ə] | *je* | wood | Resembles [ø] but is much shorter: mute "e." |

1.2.2 Nasal Vowels

Phonetic Symbol	French Example	English Approx.	Remarks
1. [ɑ̃]	*sans*	on	Say "on" with your mouth open.
2. [ɛ̃]	*pain*	can	Say "can" with your mouth open.
3. [ɔ̃]	*bon*	own	Say "own" with your mouth open.
4. [œ̃]	*un*	fun	Say "fun" with your mouth open.

Remember this little phrase, which includes all the nasal vowels: *Un bon vin blanc* [œ̃ bɔ̃ vɛ̃ blɑ̃]. A good white wine.

Denasalization, or **oral** pronunciation, of the nasal vowel occurs under **two** conditions:
1. When a nasal vowel **is followed by another "n" or "m"**: e.g., *intime* [ɛ̃tim]; *innocent* [inɔsɑ̃]; *important* [ɛ̃pɔrtɑ̃]; *immédiat* [imedja]; *enfant* [ɑ̃fɑ̃]; *ennemi* [ɛnmi]; *bon* [bɔ̃]; *bonne* [bɔn].
2. When a nasal vowel **is followed by another vowel:** e.g., *pain* [pɛ̃]; *peine* [pɛn]; *incident* [ɛ̃sidɑ̃]; *inutile* [inytil]; *profond* [prɔfɔ̃]; *chronique* [krɔnik].

1.2.3 Semi-Vowels/Semi-Consonants: Half-way Between Vowels and Consonants

1. [j]   *soulier* [sulje]; *bien* [bjɛ̃]; *hier* [jɛr]. ([j] is like biblical "Yea.")

3

2. [w] *mois* [mwa]; *Louis* [lwi]; *ouest* [wɛst]; *ouïr* [wir] (to hear); *soir* [swar].
3. [ɥ] *huit* [ɥit]; *lui* [lɥi]; *cuisine* [kɥizin]. (Based on [y] + [i]; very closed.)

1.2.4 Consonants

Pronounce them softly!

Bi-labials: [p], [b], [m]. Both lips are used. *Papa, bébé, maman.*

Labio-dentals: [f], [v]. Teeth against lower lip. *Frère, vie.*

Dentals: [t], [d], [n], [l]. Put your tongue against the back of your upper teeth to soften the sound. Don't "explode" it! *Ton, de, non, la.*

Alveolars: [ʃ], [ʒ]. Air is forced between upper and lower teeth. [ʃ] *chanson, riche, acheter;* [ʒ] *Jean, Giverny, voyage.* In English: **she**, plea**s**ure.

Palatal: [ɲ] "N" + yuh. *Champagne, Allemagne.* In English: He'll trai**n yuh.**

Velars: [k], [g]. Produced in the throat; make them soft. [k] *avec, qui, klaxon;* [g] *grand, fatigué.*

Uvular: [r]. Gargle it! *rue, Robert, travail.*

1.2.5 Spelling Groups

Phonetic symbols and examples of some common **spelling** combinations:

[e] é = *école;* ée = *fiancée;* ef = *clef* or *clé;* er = *chanter;* es = *ces;* et = *cadet;* ez = *nez;* ai = *j'ai;* e + il or ille = *pareil, merveille;* ay = *ayons.*

[ɛ] ai + consonant = *aide, aile, j'aime, palais, caisse, chaise, paix, faites;* è = *père; chèque, mène, achète, Thèbes, mèche, il lève;* ê = *tête, même, guêpe* (wasp), *gêne* (embarrassment), *chaîne;* e + tte = *dette;* e + l or lle = *sel, elle;* e + ige = *neige;* e + ine = *peine.*

[i] *ami, il y a.*

[o] *tôt, sauce, beau, ôter* [ote], *haut.*

[ɔ] *porte, observe* (most words with initial "o" are pronounced [ɔ]).

4

[œ] *coeur, peur, jeune, beurre, seul, deuil* [dœj], *boeuf.*
[u] *trou, toute, vous.*
[y] *vue, rhume* [rym], *utile* [ytil].
[ə] *je, demain, menace* [mənas], *fenêtre* [fənɛtrə].

1.3 The French Alphabet

Here is the phonetic pronunciation of the French alphabet:

Letter	Name	As in...
a	[a]	*parc*
b	[be]	*belle*
c	[se]	*ici*
d	[de]	*dame*
e	[ə]	*école* = [ekɔl]; *père* = [pɛr]; *le* – [lə]
f	[ɛf]	*fulre*
g[1]	[ʒe]	*gare; gomme; guerre; général; gilet*
h[2]	[aʃ]	*habiter* = [abite]; **héros* = ['ero]. The * and ' indicate an aspirate "h," one which is not linked to a preceding consonant.
i	[i]	*idée; imiter* = [imite]; *inégal* = [inegal]; *ici; il y a; innocent* = [inɔsã]; *mystérieux*
j[1]	[ʒi]	*jeune*
k	[ka]	*kilo.* Very few French words begin with "k"; most that do are borrowed foreign words.
l	[ɛl]	*laver; ville[3]* = [vil]; *famille* = [famij]
m	[ɛm]	*mardi; ami*
n	[ɛn]	*noble; initial; animé*
o	[o]	*dormir; oeuf* = [œf]
p	[pe]	*papa*
q	[ky]	*question* = [kɛstjɔ̃]
r	[ɛr]	*rire; pardon; irréel*
s	[ɛs]	*salle* = [sal]; *rester* = [rɛste]; *lisse* = [lis]: Initial "s;" "s" before a

		consonant, and double "s" are pronounced "s." *Plaisir* = [plezir]: "s" between two vowels = [z].
t	[te]	*tête; fait*[4]
u	[y]	*utile; tu*
v	[ve]	*voix* = [vwa]; *arriver*
w	[dubləve]	*walkman* = [wɔkman]; *wagon* = [vagɔ̃]. Many foreign words with an initial "w" are used in French. Some are pronounced "v" and some "w."
x	[ix]	Relatively few words have this initial letter.
y	[igrɛk]	Relatively few words have this initial letter.
z	[zɛd]	Relatively few words have this initial letter.

Note:

[1] "G" and "J": "g" is called [ʒe] (like "jay" in English) and "j" is called [ʒi] like "gee" in English. Remember that the names of these two letters are the opposite of what they are in the English alphabet.

[2] Aspirate "h" is not linked to a preceding consonant. Consider *"les héros"* [leero]; if you link these words, the result is [lezero] *("les zéros")* and that is certainly not the usual intention when talking about heroes!

[3] Three words and their derivatives that end in *"-ille"* are pronounced [il]: *mille villes tranquillité* [mil vil trãkil]. Similarly pronounced are *million, milliard, village,* and *tranquilité. Lille* (the city) is also [lil].

[4] Sometimes the final "t" is pronounced: *C'est un fait.* [fet] or [fe].

1.4 Accents

Accents are used in French to indicate pronunciation of vowels or to differentiate between homonyms (two words that sound alike but have different meanings, e.g., *où/ou; la/là*).

é = *accent aigu* (acute) is used only on closed "e" [e]: *éléphant, médecin* [medsɛ̃], *j'ai chanté, je suis désolé.*

è = *accent grave* is used to give the sound of open "e" [ɛ] to a mute "e" [ə] that stands before a consonant and is followed by another mute "e": *père, sèche, Hélène, j'achète, deuxième.*

à, ù = *accent grave* is used to make a distinction between two words that are spelled alike but have different meanings: *à Paris/Pierre **a** une voiture. **La** femme/**là**-bas* (over there); *Où est Jean?/Marie **ou** Simone* (or).

ç = *cédille* is used only on a "c" so it is pronounced [s] before "a," "o," and "u": *ça, garçon, Je suis déçu.*

ä, ë, ï, ö, ü = *le tréma* is used on the second vowel when two vowels occur together, to indicate that they are to be pronounced separately: *haïr* [air]; *aïeux* [ajø]; *Noël.*

1.5   Liaison

Liaison or linking occurs in speaking when a final consonant precedes an initial vowel or an "h": *cet homme; vous êtes; ils ont* [ilzɔ̃] (not to be confused with *ils sont); nos amies; un anniversaire; un bel arbre; le bouc émissaire; un grand orchestre; un patron ambitieux.*

1.5.1   Some Liaisons are to be Avoided

- Never link *"et"* to a following vowel: *Un chapeau et/un livre.*
- Never link a final "s" to an aspirate "h": *les/hors-d'oeuvre* [le ɔrdœvrə].
- But do link the "h" in: *un hôpital, l'homme, des huîtres*, etc.
- In inversions, don't link the final "s" of the plural to a following vowel: *Avez-vous/une soeur? Vont-ils/en Europe? Sont-elles/ici?* In fact, the tendency among many young French speakers today is to avoid liaison, except where it is necessary for comprehension.

1.6   Elision

When final and initial vowels come together, the final vowel is replaced by an apostrophe: *l'amie, c'est; l'examen; il n'est pas; l'heure; Est-ce qu'il faut parler?*

"Si" is elided before "i" but not before the other vowels: *s'il vous plaît; si elle accepte; si on arrive,* etc.

Exceptions: *le huit octobre; le onze février, tu as, tu es, Le Havre.*

1.7   Syllabification

A French syllable is determined by the vowel within it: *é-té; a-mi; dé-ter-mi-ner; ré-pé-ti-tion; in-di-vi-du,* etc. When you wish to separate a word, either do so at the vowel itself or if there is a double consonant, make the separation between the two letters: *fi-nis-sez; lit-té-ra-ture; syl-la-be,* etc.

CHAPTER 2

Cognates — Words You Recognize

Many words are common to both French and English; others have slight spelling differences and still others have familiar characteristics which help to identify their meaning.

2.1 Cognates Common to Both Languages

restaurant	dessert	menu	service	table
art	culture	film	statue	tennis
football	sport	machine	science	client
magazine	concert	piano	cousin	parents
rouge	rose	violet	orange	automobile
route	train	promenade	taxi	suite
voyage	probable	possible	solitude	surprise
courage	brave	moment	content	secret

2.2 Cognates with Minor Spelling Changes

musique	mémoire	professeur	leçon	classe
magique	saison	sophistiqué	artiste	poème
allée	répéter	théâtre	auteur	poète
acteur	actrice	comédie	tragédie	première
opéra	chambre	bleu	pourpre	touriste

9

élégant	*difficulté*	*hôtel*	*président*	*congrès*
sénateur	*élection*	*gouvernement*	*voter*	*distingué*
démocratie	*américain*	*nationalité*	*loyauté*	*telévision*

2.3 Spelling Pitfalls

These common words are spelled differently from their English cognates and may cause confusion:

exemple	*indépendant*	*mariage*	*appartement*	*médecin*
rythme	*rime*	*littérature*	*revue*	*peintre*
personne	*intéressant*	*fascinant*	*automne*	*erreur*
exercice	*douzaine*	*dictionnaire*	*couleur*	*danseur*
thé	*riz*	*chrysanthème*	*succès*	*procès*
adresse	*calendrier*	*personnage*	*oignon*	*carotte*
omelette	*mathématiques*			

2.4 *"Faux amis"* (False Friends)

The following cognates seem to mean one thing in English but really mean something quite different in French:

à l'heure actuelle – at the present time

les actualités – the news

actuellement – now

en réalité – actually

assister – to attend

attendre – to wait for

se douter de – to suspect

sans doute – probably

ignorer – to be unaware of

large – broad, wide

bague – ring

sac – bag, purse

une occasion – an opportunity, a chance

place – a square (Place Vendôme) or a seat at the theatre, on the bus, etc.

regarder – to look at, to gaze at

chargé – loaded, burdened

crier – to shout or yell

rester – to stay or remain

sensible – sensitive, keen senses

sensiblement – approximately

canapé – sofa, couch

librairie – book store

bibliothèque – library

un roman – a novel

journée – all day long

voyage – a journey	*voyager* – to travel
quitter – to leave	*travailler* – to work

2.5 Some Borrowed Words

Some words that have been borrowed from French have been "Americanized," in that their pronunciation has changed somewhat. These words include:

lingerie	*chaise longue*	*quai*	*maître d'hôtel*
femme	*à la mode*	*salon*	*hors-d'oeuvre*
foyer	*billet-doux*	*à la carte*	*grand prix*
chef-d'oeuvre	*tête-a-tête*	*rendez-vous*	*café*
haute couture	*chauffeur*	*garage*	*cuisine*
croissant	*vinaigrette*	*détente*	*coup d'état*
chiffon	*mot-clef*	*tour de force*	*liaison*
de luxe	*exposé*	*gourmet*	*rouge*
au pair	*chic*	*coup de grâce*	*fiancé(e)*
beau	*soufflé*	*voilà*	*fait accompli*
fête	*idiot savant*	*suite*	*raison d'être*
en garde	*ballet*	*pas de deux*	*entrepreneur*

French has borrowed many words from English, too. (It's *"le franglais"* that purists deplore!)

le week-end	*le parking*	*faire le shopping*
les fast-foods	*le steak*	*le jet-set*
un job	*"cool"*	*"super-cool"*
les spots télévisés	*faire du foot*	*les stars*
le rock et roll	*le marketing*	*le business*
le budget	*un manager*	*le "look"*
la "pub" [licité]	*le tunnel*	*un building de haut standing*
un superman	*un speaker*	*une speakerine*

2.6 Capitalization

Fewer words are capitalized in French than in English. Important examples are:

"Je" is capitalized only when it begins a sentence: *Je suis son ami.* But: *Ce matin je vais rester ici. Elle sait que je veux partir. Que sais-je? Il faut que je te parle.*

Names of languages are not capitalized: *le français, le chinois, le russe, l'italien, l'anglais, le grec, l'allemand, le japonais.*

Days of the week and months of the year are not capitalized: *lundi, mardi, mercredi, dimanche; janvier, avril, décembre.*

Nationalities of people or national origins of things (adjectives) are not capitalized: *Vous êtes américain(e). Elle a une voiture danoise. J'aime la cuisine chinoise. Gildas est breton* (from Brittany). *Margot porte une robe parisienne.*

Nationalities (people) are capitalized: *Les Suisses font du chocolat magnifique. Connais-tu des Français? On croit que les Américains sont riches. Les Canadiens sont nos voisins. Nous avons rencontré beaucoup d'Européens.*

Names of cities, states, provinces, countries, rivers, oceans, mountains, and continents are capitalized: *Londres, la Californie, la Normandie, l'Italie, les Etats-Unis, l'Asie, l'Australie, la Seine, l'Atlantique, les Alpes.*

Capitalization varies for the titles of books, films, or plays: Generally the article is not capitalized but the first noun is: *l'Etranger; les Misérables; le Rouge et le noir; les Fleurs du mal.* But when the first word is not an article, only that word is capitalized: *Lettres de mon moulin; Tous les matins du monde; Autant en emporte le vent* (Gone with the Wind). When the title is a clause and begins with a definite article, that is the capitalized word: *Les dieux ont soif; La guerre de Troie n'aura pas lieu; Le deuil sied à Electra* (Mourning Becomes Electra).

CHAPTER 3

By The Numbers

3.1   Counting from 1 to 1,000,000,000

The French numerical system becomes somewhat complicated when you arrive at the 70's, 80's, and 90's. Otherwise the pattern of counting is regular:

un	[œ̃]	1	onze	[ɔ̃z]	11
deux	[dø]	2	douze	[duz]	12
trois	[trwa]	3	treize	[trɛz]	13
quatre	[katrə]	4	quatorze	[katɔrz]	14
cinq	[sɛ̃k]	5	quinze	[kɛ̃z]	15
six	[sis]	6	seize	[sɛz]	16
sept	[sɛt]	7	dix-sept	[disɛt]	17
huit	[ɥit]	8	dix-huit	[dizɥit]	18
neuf	[nœf]	9	dix-neuf	[diznœf]	19
dix	[dis]	10	vingt	[vɛ̃]	20

vingt et un	21	vingt-sept	27
vingt-deux	22	vingt-huit	28
vingt-trois	23	vingt-neuf	29
vingt-quatre	24	trente [trãt]	30
vingt-cinq	25		
vingt-six	26		

Continue the same pattern with:

trente et un, trente-deux, etc.   31, 32, …
quarante, quarante et un, quarante-deux, etc. 40, 41, 42,…
cinquante, cinquante et un, cinquante-deux, etc. 50, 51, 52,…

Note: Continue with **soixante, soixante et un** (60, 61) until you reach **soixante-neuf** (69). Now you will say 60 + 10, **soixante-dix,** for 70. Once you say **"dix,"** continue with **"onze,"** so that you say:

soixante-dix	70	*soixante-quinze*	75
soixante et onze	71	*soixante-seize*	76
soixante-douze	72	*soixante-dix-sept*	77
soixante-treize	73	*soixante-dix-huit*	78
soixante-quatorze	74	*soixante-dix-neuf*	79

Now you are going to **multiply: 4×20 = *quatre* $\times$ *vingts* = quatre-vingts** (80). Note that there is an *"s"* in **quatre-vingts** and that there is **no *"s"*** and **no *"et"*** in **quatre-vingt-un** (81).
Now continue with **"–deux":**

quatre-vingt-deux	82	*quatre-vingt-six*	86
quatre-vingt-trois	83	*quatre-vingt-sept*	87
quatre-vingt-quatre	84	*quatre-vingt-huit*	88
quatre-vingt-cinq	85	*quatre-vingt-neuf*	89

And now you say: $4 \times 20 + 10$ = **quatre-vingt-dix** (90). Now continue with **"onze"** once again:

quatre-vingt-onze	91	*quatre-vingt-seize*	96
quatre-vingt-douze	92	*quatre-vingt-dix-sept*	97
quatre-vingt-treize	93	*quatre-vingt-dix-huit*	98
quatre-vingt-quatorze	94	*quatre-vingt-dix-neuf*	99
quatre-vingt-quinze	95		

cent	100	*deux cent un* (No *"s"*)	201
cent un (No *"et"*) [saœ̃]	101	*trois cents*	300
deux cents	200		

14

quatre cents, cinq cents, six cents, sept cents, huit cents, neuf cents
mille [mil]   1.000

Note: **French** uses a **period** (.) where **English** uses a **comma** (,)
to denote **thousands** or **millions.** Also, a **comma** (,) is used in **French**
where **English** uses a **period** (.), as in **decimals:** *2,75* (Fr.) = 2.75
(Eng.); *,55* = .55; *,0426* = .0426, etc.

deux mille (No "s")	2.000
deux mille un	2.001
trois mille	3.000
etc.	
un million [miljɔ̃]	1.000.000
deux million (No "s")	2.000.000
etc.	
un milliard [miljar], billion	1.000.000.000

3.2   Telling Time

Quelle heure est-il? What time is it? *Il est...* It is...
une heure = 1h = 1:00
une heure cinq = 1h5 = 1:05
une heure dix = 1h10 = 1:10
une heure et quart = 1h15 = 1:15
une heure vingt = 1h20 = 1:20
une heure et demie = 1h30 =1:30

Note: *"et"* is used only for the **quarter** and **half-hour.**

After the ½ hour, you start to **subtract** from the following hour:

deux heures moins vingt-cinq = 1h35 = 1:35
deux heures moins vingt = 1h40 = 1:40 (or twenty-to-two)
deux heures moins le quart = 1h45 = 1:45 (the definite article
    "le" is used only for this measure of time.)
deux heures = 2h = 2:00
midi (cf. mid-day) = 12 noon   *minuit* = 12 p.m.

The French often denote the hours between noon and midnight in "official" time; this is especially true when referring to the time of appointments, films, concerts, programs, etc. For example, *quatorze heures* (14h) = 2 p.m.; *vingt heures* (20h) = 8 p.m.; etc. Midnight is *vingt-quatre heures.*

Hint: Subtract 12 from the official time to get p.m. time.

3.3 Describing Time

Ways of talking about time:

Quelle est la date aujourd'hui? What's today's date?
Quel jour sommes-nous? What day is it?
C'est le 15 avril. It's April 15.
C'est mardi, le 15 avril. It's Tuesday, April 15.
C'est le 15 aujourd'hui. It's the 15th today.
On est le quinze. It's the 15th.
C'est le quinze avril, mille neuf cent quatre-vingt-quatorze. It's
    April 15, 1994.

3.4 Days of the Week

Les jours de la semaine: lundi, mardi, mercredi, jeudi, vendredi, samedi, dimanche. The days of the week, Monday, Tuesday, etc., are not capitalized in French.

Note: The French week begins on **Monday,** rather than Sunday.

Hint: Never say *"à" lundi, "en" lundi,* or *"sur" lundi* for **on** Monday; the day of the week alone is sufficient:

*Je verrai Pierre **lundi.*** I'll see Peter **on Monday.**
*Margo est arrivée **mardi.*** Margo arrived **on Tuesday.**
*Nous allons partir **jeudi.*** We're leaving **on Thursday.**

For the **day in general** use the definite article:

*Elle travaille **le lundi** jusqu'à minuit.* **Mondays** she works until

16

midnight.

Le mercredi ils se rencontrent en ville. They meet in town **on Wednesday(s).**

Les enfants n'aiment pas le dimanche. Children don't like **Sundays.**

3.5 Months

The months are very similar to their English cognates but are **not capitalized:** *janvier, février, mars, avril, mai, juin, juillet, août, septembre, octobre, novembre, décembre.*

Quand est votre anniversaire? When is your birthday?

C'est le 25 mai. It's May 25.

Je suis né(e) le 13 octobre. I was born on October 13.

Mon anniversaire, c'est le premier août. My birthday is August 1st.

Quelle est la date de la fête nationale américaine? When is America's national holiday?

C'est le 4 juillet. It's July 4th.

3.6 The Four Seasons: *Les quatre saisons*

Le printemps, l'été, l'automne, l'hiver. Spring, summer, autumn (note French spelling change), winter.

In autumn = *en automne; en hiver, en été,* but *au printemps,* because the preposition now precedes a **consonant.**

3.7 Expressing the Year

You may use either form:

1492	*mille quatre cent quatre-vingt-douze* or
	quatorze cent quatre-vingt-douze
1776	*mille sept cent soixante-seize* or
	dix-sept cent soixante-seize
1812	*mille huit cent douze* or
	dix-huit cent douze

1994	*mille neuf cent quatre-vingt-quatorze* or
	dix-neuf cent quatre-vingt-quatorze
2001	*deux mille un*

3.8   Phone Numbers

Quel est votre numéro de téléphone? What's your phone number?

US: (219) 468-9876. *Indicatif régional: deux cent dix-neuf. Quatre cent soixante-huit, quatre-vingt dix-huit, soixante-seize.* Area code: two hundred nineteen. Four hundred sixty-eight, ninety-eight, seventy-six.

French numbers are quoted in four pairs; a typical number in the Paris area is (1) 60.42.27.99. *Composer le un* (Dial 1), *soixante, quarante-deux, vingt-sept, quatre-vingt-dix-neuf.*

3.9   Expressing Age

To talk about **age,** use *"avoir":*

Quel âge avez-vous? How old are you?

J'ai 23 ans. I'm 23.

Ma soeur a 25 et mes parents ont 47. My sister's 25 and my parents are 47.

La France a plus de mille ans. France is more than 1,000 years old.

3.10   Calculations

For **addition, subtraction, multiplication,** and **division:**

$2 + 2 = 4$	*Deux **plus** deux **font** quatre*
$10 - 3 = 7$	*Dix **moins** trois **égale** sept*
$20 \times 2 = 40$	*Vingt **fois** deux **font** quarante*
$10 \div 5 = 2$	*Dix **divisé** par cinq **égale** deux*

3.11   Comparisons

Comparisons of **equality, inferiority,** and **superiority** are made by using the following structures:

3.11.1 Equality

*Jean a deux soeurs; Pierre a deux soeurs. Jean a **autant de soeurs** que Pierre.* John has two sister.; Pierre has two sisters. John has **as many** sisters as Peter.

*Marie-France gagne 3.000 francs par mois; Simone gagne le même salaire. Simone gagne **autant d'argent que** Marie-France.* Marie-France earns 3,000 francs a month; Simone earns the same salary. Simone earns **as much** money as Marie-France.

autant de + noun + *que* = comparison of equality: as much as, as many as...

3.11.2 Inferiority

*Nous visitons trente villes; vous visitez trente-deux villes. Nous vistons **moins de villes que** vous.* We visit thirty cities; you visit thirty two cities. We visit **less cities than** you.

*Les Duval boivent trois bouteilles de vin mais leurs cousins n'en boivent que deux. Leurs cousins boivent **moins de vin que** les Duval.* The Duvals drink three bottles of wine but their cousins only drink two. Their cousins drink **less wine than** the Duvals.

moins de + noun + *que* = less than (singular or plural quantity).

3.11.3 Superiority

*Robert a dix-huit livres; tu as quinze livres. Il a **plus de livres** que toi.* Robert has eighteen books; you have fifteen books. He has more books than you (do).

*Margot passe trois jours à Paris; sa mère y passe cinq jours. Sa mère passe **plus de temps** à Paris **que** Margot.* Margot spends three days in Paris; her mother spends five days. Her mother spends more time in Paris than Margot.

plus de + noun + *que* = more than (singular or plural quantity).

3.11.4 Generalized Comparisons

For comparisons that do not entail numbers but are more **generalized** comparisons, use *autant que, moins que, plus que:*

*Tu lis **autant que** moi.* You read as much as I do.
*Paul parle **moins que** son père.* Paul talks less than his father (does).
*Elise voyage **plus que** sa soeur.* Elise travels more than her sister.

3.12 Ordinal Numbers

To express numbers that represent **consecutive order** (first, tenth, twenty-first, thirtieth, etc.) use:

premier, première	first (m. & f.)
deuxième	second
troisième	third
quatrième	fourth
cinquième	fifth
vingt et unième	twenty-first
etc.	

Note: While the English form of these numbers varies, aside from *premier,* French uses the suffix *"—ième"* for **all numbers.**

Dates are expressed by **cardinal** numbers: *le cinq mai, le vingt-deux septembre, le trente juillet,* even though English uses **ordinal** numbers: the 5th of May, the 22nd of September, July 30th, etc.
Exception: The first day of the month is expressed by the **ordinal** form: *le premier juin, le premier décembre,* etc.

CHAPTER 4

Nouns and Articles

4.1 Gender

French nouns are either masculine or feminine. Although many feminine nouns end in "e," there are too many exceptions to this rule to make it reliable. However, certain endings may help you to identify whether a word is of the masculine or feminine gender, although there are also several exceptions to the rule.

4.1.1 Masculine Nouns

Nouns which refer to **masculine beings,** both humans and animals:

l'homme, le garçon, le prince, l'empereur, le roi, le duc, le mâle, le cheval, le coq, etc.

Guide to Identifying Masculine Nouns

Ending of Noun	Examples	Exceptions
"—age"	*l'âge*	*une image*
	le fromage	*une cage*
	le nuage	*la plage*
	un étage	*une page*
	Quel dommage!	

Ending of Noun	Examples	Exceptions
"—*eur*"	*un professeur*	*la faveur*
	le docteur	*une rumeur*
	un auteur	*la chaleur*
	un ordinateur	
	le bonheur	
	l'extérieur	
"—*isme*"	*le capitalisme*	
	le patriotisme	
	le socialisme	
	le féminisme	
	l'impressionnisme	
"—*ment*"	*l'appartement*	
	le département	
	les renseignements	
	un compliment	
	le médicament	
	les vêtements	
Vowels other than [ə]	*le cinéma*	*la radio*
	le trou	*l'eau*
	le piano	*la vertu*
	le bureau	
	le café	
	le hibou	
Consonant	*le raisin*	*la saison*
	le jour	*l'amour*
	le nez	*la clef*
	le doigt	*la nuit*
	le champ	*la mort*
	le ciel	

Ending of Noun	Examples	Exceptions
Foreign words	*le pique-nique*	*une interview*
	le bifteck	
	le weekend	
	le marketing	
	le base-ball	
	le parking	

The names of languages are masculine: *le français, le russe, le japonais,* etc.

4.1.2   Feminine Nouns

Nouns that are used to describe **female beings,** both humans and animals:

la femme, une fille, une mère, une tante, la nièce, la reine, la princesse, la poule, la vache, la chatte, la chienne

Guide to Identifying Feminine Nouns

Ending of Noun	Examples	Exceptions
"—ade"	*une promenade*	
	une tirade	
	la limonade	
"—ance" or	*la naissance*	*le silence*
"—ence"	*la distance*	
	l'indépendance	
	la différence	
	la patience	
	la science	
"—oire"	*la gloire*	*le mémoire –*
	l'histore	(student paper)
	une poire	
	la victoire	
	la mémoire	

Ending of Noun	Examples	Exceptions
"—sion" or "—tion"	*une impression* *une décision* *la télévision* *la libération* *une condition* *une répétition* *la constitution*	
"—son"	*la saison* *une maison* *la raison* *la liaison* *une chanson*	*le son*
"—é" or "—ée"	*la pensée* *l'idée* *la liberté* *l'égalité* *la bonté*	*le comité*

4.1.3 Feminine Nouns/Masculine Beings

Some **feminine** nouns can refer to **masculine** beings:

*Philippe ést **la sentinelle** ce soir.* Philip is the sentry tonight.
*Georges était **une victime** de l'épidémie.* George was a victim of the epidemic.
*Henri est **une personne** importante.* Henry is an important person.

4.1.4 Masculine Nouns/Feminine Beings

Some **masculine** nouns can refer to **feminine** beings:

*Elle est **écrivain**.* She's a writer. (or) *C'est une femme **écrivain**.*
*Le **soprano** était magnifique.* The soprano was wonderful.
*Mon **professeur** est une femme intelligente.* My professor is an intelligent woman.

4.1.5 Identical Forms/Different Meanings

Some nouns have identical masculine and feminine forms but different meanings:

Masculine		Feminine	
un livre	a book	*une livre*	a pound
le page	a page-boy	*la page*	a page
le tour	a turn	*une tour*	a tower
le vase	a vase	*la vase*	mud or sludge
le critique	the critic	*la critique*	criticism

4.2 Formation of Feminine Nouns

Many feminine nouns are formed by adding "e" to the masculine:

l'ami/l'amie; le cousin/la cousine; un voisin/une voisine; le berger/la bergère; l'étudiant/l'étudiante

4.2.1 Irregular Feminine Noun Forms

Masculine	Feminine	Exceptions
le vendeur	*la vendeuse*	
le danseur	*la danseuse*	
le menteur	*la menteuse*	
un coiffeur	*une coiffeuse*	*l'acteur/l'actrice*
		le directeur/la directrice
		un lecteur/une lectrice

4.2.2 Variant Forms

Some feminine nouns are quite different from their masculine counterparts:

Masculine	Feminine
le père	*la mère*
le frère	*la soeur*
l'homme	*la femme* (woman)
le mari	*la femme* (wife)
un dieu	*une déesse*
le roi	*la reine*
un neveu	*une nièce*
un oncle	*une tante*
un héros	*une héroïne*
le gendre	*la belle-fille*
un coq	*une poule*
un cerf	*une biche*

4.2.3   Same Form for Masculine and Feminine

Some nouns use the same form for describing both male and female:

> *un/une enfant; un/une artiste; un/une camarade; un/une esclave; un/une philosophe; un/une secrétaire,* etc.

4.3   Plural Nouns

Normally, as in English, the plural of nouns is formed by adding an "s" to the singular:

> *le stylo/les stylos; la table/les tables; l'arbre/les arbres; l'ami/les amis* and *l'amie/les amies,* etc.

4.3.1   Nouns Ending in "s," "x," or "z"

Nouns that end in "s," "x," or "z" do not add "s" for the plural:

> *le repas/les repas; la croix/les croix; le nez/les nez*

4.3.2 Some Irregular Plural Nouns

Singular Ending	Plural	Exceptions
—al, —ail:		
journal	*journaux*	*bals*
animal	*animaux*	*récitals*
cheval	*chevaux*	*carnavals*
canal	*canaux*	*festivals*
métal	*métaux*	*chacals*
mal	*maux*	
vitrail	*vitraux*	*chandails*
travail	*travaux*	*détails*
—au, —eu, —eau:		
noyau	*noyaux*	*pneus*
eau	*eaux*	
neveu	*neveux*	
niveau	*niveaux*	
—ou: Most take "s" in the plural		**7 exceptions:**
fou	*fous*	*bijoux*
cou	*cous*	*cailloux*
sou	*sous*	*choux*
trou	*trous*	*genoux*
		hiboux
		joujoux
		poux

4.3.3 Three Plural Nouns that are Very Irregular

un oeil / des yeux – an eye / eyes
le ciel / les cieux – sky, as in weather / Heaven
le jeune homme / les jeunes gens – young man / young folks

Note: *"ciels"* is also used in poetry and in discussing paintings; e.g., *"les ciels de Gaugin."*

4.3.4 Three Feminine Nouns that are Always Plural

les mathématiques (often shortened to *"les maths"*)
les vacances
les fiançailles

4.3.5 Family Names

Family names do not change in the plural form except for those of royal dynasties:

les Duval – the Duvals; *les Mitterrand* – the Mitterrands
but:
les Bourbons, les Plantagenêts

4.3.6 Plural of Compound Nouns

Some compound nouns contain verbs and adverbs which are invariable. Nouns and adjectives are sometimes pluralized.

Singular	Plural
un gratte-ciel	*des gratte-ciel* ("sky" is singular)
une pomme de terre	*des pommes de terre* ("earth" is singular)
un coffre-fort	*des coffres-forts*
un arc-en-ciel	*des arcs-en-ciel*
un chef-d'oeuvre	*des chefs-d'oeuvre*

Check the dictionary to be sure of the correct plural form of compound nouns.

4.4 The Article

The article introduces the noun and may be definite or indefinite. **It is usually repeated before each noun.** Although in English we often omit articles, in French the noun must always be preceded by an article.

4.4.1 Definite Articles: "The"

	Masculine	Feminine
Singular	*le garçon*	*la femme*
	le billet	*la maison*
	le soir	*la plage*
Plural	*les garçons*	*les femmes*
	les billets	*les maisons*
	les soirs	*les plages*

Note: When a singular noun begins with a vowel, the article becomes *l'*:

	Masculine	Feminine
	l'ami	*l'amie*
	l'aéroport	*l'école*
	l'oeil	*l'usine*

4.4.2 Repetition of the Article

Articles are generally repeated before each noun in a series:

J'ai invité tout le monde: la mère, le fils, la fille, l'oncle, et les cousins. I invited everyone: mother, son, daughter, uncle, and cousins.

4.4.3 Contractions with an Article

After the prepositions *"à"* and *"de"* (at the, to the, in the, of the, from the), some forms of the definite article become contractions:

$$
\begin{aligned}
à + la &= à\ la \\
à + le &= au \\
à + l' &= à\ l' \\
à + les &= aux
\end{aligned}
$$

Nous sommes allés à l'ecole. We went to the school.
Nous avons parlé à la secrétaire. We spoke to the secretary.

*Au début de la semaine, il écrira **aux** clients.* At the beginning
of the week, he'll write to the customers.
*Il fera beau **au** printemps.* It will be nice [weather] in [the] spring.

de + la	=	de la
de + le	=	du
de + l'	=	de l'
de + les	=	des

*Jean est le père **de l'**enfant.* John is the father of the child.
*As-tu appris les paroles **de la** chanson?* Did you learn the words
of the song?
*C'est le plus beau pays **du** monde, le pays **des** merveilles.* It's the
most beautiful country in the world, the land of marvels.
*Ils reviennent **du** sud.* They're returning from the south.

4.5   Special Uses of the Definite Article

The definite article is used to make generalized observations:

Les voitures de sport sont chères. Sports cars are expensive.
Les oiseaux mangent tout le temps. Birds eat constantly.

Note: In English we often omit the article in these kinds of state-
ments.

4.5.1   The Definite Article with *aimer, préférer, adorer, détester*

An easy acronym is "A PAD."
Since these four verbs express one's **general** feeling about a person, place or thing, they **always** take the definite article.

*Nous **aimons les films** français.* We like French films.
*Laure **adore la vanille** mais elle **déteste le chocolat**.* Laura loves
vanilla but hates chocolate.
*Préfères-tu **le bleu** ou **le rouge**?* Do you prefer blue or red?

4.5.2 With Titles, Professions, and Countries

The definite article is used when addressing or describing titled or important individuals:

Titles:
le président, **la** *comtesse,* **le** *sénateur,* etc.
Oui, monsieur **le** *Président.* **Le** *Président Mitterrand a parlé.*
Yes, Mr. President. President Mitterrand spoke.

Professions:
Le *docteur Duval est arrivé.* Doctor Duval has arrived.

Countries: "Feminine" countries (i.e., those whose final letter is *"e"*) are preceded by the definite article when they are the **subject** or **direct object** of the verb:

La *France est belle.* France is beautiful.
J'ai visité **l'Italie** *et* **la Belgique.** I visited Italy and Belgium.

Use *"le"* for **"masculine" countries** (those which end in a consonant):

Le Japon *exporte beaucoup de produits électroniques.* Japan exports a lot of electronic products.
Elles vont visiter **le Danemark** *et* **le Brésil.** They will visit Denmark and Brazil.

Exceptions:
1. **Le Mexique.** Mexico.
2. No article is used when discussing islands: *Tahiti est très beau.* Tahiti is very beautiful.
3. No article is used before Israel: *Ils connaissent bien* **Israel.** They know Israel well.

"Les" is used for plural countries:

31

Les Etats-Unis. The United States.
Les Pays-Bas. The Netherlands.

4.6   The Indefinite Article

The indefinite articles "a," "an," "some," "any" are used to refer to a non-specific noun.

Masculine	Feminine	Plural
un livre	*une lettre*	*des cousins*
un stylo	*une jupe*	*des lunettes*
un jardin	*une chanson*	*des bonbons*

Ils ont acheté des légumes. They bought some vegetables.
Jacques a reçu une lettre. Jack received a letter.
C'est un bon livre. It's a good book.

4.6.1   Special Uses of the Indefinite Article

Use the indefinite article to answer a question:

Qu'est-ce que c'est? What is it? (or "this")?
C'est une discussion importante. It's an important discussion.
Qui est-ce? Who is it? (or "this")?
C'est une bonne amie. She's a good friend.

Also use the indefinite article to describe a profession, or a religious or political persuasion:

Voilà Pierre. C'est un médecin célèbre. There's Peter. He's a
    famous doctor.
Mme Aumont, c'est une catholique orthodoxe. Mrs. Aumont is a
    devout Catholic.

Remember the rule: *C'est un, une, des, le, la, les* + noun **for identification.** *Ce sont* + *les* or *des* may be used for plural nouns.

CHAPTER 5

The Partitive Article
(Le Partitif)

5.1 General Use

The partitive is based on describing **"a part** of all the ... that exists in the world." While in English, "some" or "any" may be omitted, the partitive article must be expressed in French, except in certain structures.

5.2 Formation

		Partitive	Example
Masculine	*de + le*	*du*	*Voulez-vous du vin?* Do you want some/any wine?
	de + l'	*de l'*	*As-tu de l'argent?*
Feminine	*de + la*	*de la*	*Elle a acheté de la crème.* She bought some cream.
	de + l'	*de l'*	*Va-t-il dépenser de l'argent?* Is he going to spend any money?

		Partitive	Example
Plural	*de + les*	*des*	*Nous cherchons **des** livres intéressants.* We're looking for interesting books.
			*Margot a acheté **des** robes chic.* Margot bought some chic dresses.

5.3 Omission of the Definite Article after *"de"*

5.3.1 With Negative Expressions

pas de   *Simon n'a **pas d'**amis.* Simon hasn't any friends.

plus de   *Nous ne voulons **plus de** problèmes.* We don't want any more problems.

jamais de   *Il ne porte **jamais de** cravate.* He never wears a tie.

5.3.2 With Adverbs of Quantity

beaucoup de   *Elle a eu **beaucoup de** chance.* She had lots of luck.

trop de   *Manges-tu **trop de** pain?* Do you eat too much bread?

assez de   *Il n'avait pas **assez d'**argent pour le billet.* He didn't have enough money for the ticket.

un peu de   *Nous voulons **un peu de** soupe et **peu de** viande.*

peu de   We want a little soup and not much meat.

5.3.3 After Certain Expressions

avoir besoin de   *J'ai **besoin de** vacances.* I need a vacation.

avoir envie de   *As-tu **envie de** gâteau?* Do you feel like having some cake?

5.3.4 Before a Plural Noun Preceded by an Adjective

*Nous avons vu **de belles** maisons.* We saw (some) beautiful homes.

*Ce chien a **de grands yeux**.* This dog has big eyes.

5.4   Definite, Indefinite, or Partitive Article

5.4.1   The Definite Article

The definite article **describes a specific noun:**

*Nous avons visité **le musée, la tour,** et **les** vieux **bâtiments.*** We visited the museum, the tower, and the old buildings.

The definite article **makes a general observation:**

Les vitamines** sont bonnes pour **la santé. Vitamins are good for your health.

5.4.2   Indefinite Article

The indefinite article refers to a class of persons or things that are **not specifically identified:**

***Un homme** lui a parlé.* A man spoke to her.
*Nous avons lu **une histoire** triste.* We read a sad story.
*Y a-t-il **des chats** chez toi?* Are there (any) cats at your house?

5.4.3   The Partitive Article

The partitive article describes quantities that are **a part of an entire class of people or objects:**

*Nous avons rencontré **des gens intéressants.*** We met (some) interesting people.
*Il n'a pas lu beaucoup **d'articles.*** He didn't read many articles.
*Nos invités prennent **du thé** le matin.* Our guests drink tea in the morning.

5.4.4   Résumé

*--Voulez-vous **de l'eau?***
*--Non, merci, je ne veux **pas d'eau** parce que je **n'aime pas l'eau.** Je préfère **le coca.***

*--Mais **l'eau** ici est spéciale. Prenez seulement **un peu d'eau** et vous verrez.*

*--D'accord. Mais ne me donnez qu'**un petit verre d'eau** et nous resterons **de bons amis.***

"Do you want some water?"

"No, thanks, I don't want any water because I don't like water. I prefer Coke."

"But the water here is special. Have just a bit of water and you'll see."

"All right. But give me only a small glassful and we'll remain good friends."

CHAPTER 6

Adjectives

6.1 Function

Adjectives **qualify** or **describe** nouns and pronouns and may be either concrete or abstract in meaning.

C'est une grande maison. It's a large house.
C'est un examen important. It's an important exam.

6.1.1 Agreement in Gender and Number

Adjectives vary in **number** and **gender** to **agree** with the nouns they modify.

Philippe est blond et ses soeurs sont blondes aussi. Phillip is blonde and his sisters are blonde too.
La vieille église se trouve à côté d'un vieux château. The old church is situated near an old castle.
Elle porte des bas blancs et des souliers noirs. She's wearing white stockings and black shoes.

6.2 Formation of Feminine

Regular adjectives add an "e" to the masculine to make the feminine form:

petit/petite; rond/ronde; fort/forte

Adjectives that end in "e" are invariable:

une rue large; un stylo rouge; un/une autre enfant

"Chic" is also invariable:

un hôtel chic; une robe chic

6.2.1   Common Irregular Forms

There are several irregular forms:

Masculine	Feminine	Plural
un mur épais	*une tête épaisse*	*des murs épais*
un faux ami	*une fausse amie*	*de faux amis*
un esprit vif	*une couleur vive*	*des esprits vifs*
un air doux	*une chanson douce*	*des voisins doux*
un garçon malin	*une fille maligne*	*des gens malins*
un stylo favori	*une robe favorite*	*des choses favorites*
un vin sec	*une peau sèche*	*des peaux sèches*
un homme sérieux	*une femme sérieuse*	*des gens sérieux*
de l'air frais	*une idée fraîche*	*des idées fraîches*

6.3   Position of Adjectives

The majority of adjectives **follow** the noun but there are about a dozen adjectives that commonly **precede** it.

Masculine	Feminine
*un **autre** cheval*	*une **autre** personne*
*un **beau*** garçon*	*une **belle** fille*
*un **bon** livre*	*une **bonne** histoire*
*un **certain** homme*	*une **certaine** femme*
*un **grand** problème*	*une **grande** montagne*

Masculine	Feminine
un **gros** nez	une **grosse** poule
un **jeune** enfant	une **jeune** enfant
un **joli** chapeau	une **jolie** robe
un **long** chemin	une **longue** leçon
un **mauvais** jour	une **mauvaise** vie
un **nouveau*** complet	une **nouvelle** situation
un **vieux*** soldat	une **vieille** dame

* Each of these three adjectives has another form used before **masculine nouns with initial vowels:**

	beau	*nouveau*	*vieux*
Singular	bel	nouvel	vieil
Plural	beaux	nouveaux	vieux

un bel arbre – a beautiful tree
de beaux arbres – beautiful trees
un nouvel endroit – a new place
de nouveaux endroits – new places
un viel état – an old state
de vieux états – old states

Remember that the correct form of the plural is *de grandes montagnes, de jolis chapeaux, etc.*

6.3.1 Before or After a Noun with the Same Meaning

Many adjectives may be placed before or after the noun for stylistic effect, **without a change in meaning:**

Joyeux Noël/une aventure joyeuse; une merveilleuse surprise/ une occasion merveilleuse

6.3.2 Change in Position, Change in Meaning

Some adjectives may change meaning with a change in position:

un pauvre enfant – a poor child
un enfant pauvre – a child without money

un professeur ancien – an aged teacher
un ancien professeur – a former teacher

une brave personne – a good person (in character)
une personne brave – a courageous person

mon cher oncle – my dear uncle
ma voiture chère – my expensive car

un grand homme – a great man (famous, important)
un homme grand – a tall man

le même jour – the same day
le jour même – the very day

*Nous arrivons **le même jour** que toi.* We're arriving the same
   day as you are.
*Il est parti **le jour même** de son mariage.* He left on the very day
   of his wedding.

le mois dernier – last month (compared to this month)
le dernier mois – the last month (in a series)

*Décembre est **le dernier mois** de l'année.* December is the last
   month of the year.

propre – showing possession
propre – clean

*Elle utilise **sa propre voiture.*** She uses her own car.
*Cette **maison propre** est admirable.* This clean house is admirable.

certain – a vague number
certain – sure

Certaines *gens* sont impolis.* Some people are impolite.
Son voyage est **certain.** His trip is a sure thing.

* Note: *"gens"* is **feminine** when it has an adjective **preceding** it and **masculine** when it has an adjective **following** it: *de bonnes gens; des gens heureux.*

6.3.3   Adjectives of Color

Most adjectives of color are placed after the noun and form the feminine by adding "e":

vert/verte; gris/grise; noir/noire

Note these exceptions:

un ciel **bleu**	*une cravate* **bleue**	*des livres* **bleus**
un chien **blanc**	*une chemise* **blanche**	
un ruban **violet**	*une veste* **violette**	
un crayon **marron**	*une table* **marron***	*des cheveux* **marron**

Note: *Marron* (chestnut brown) is a noun and therefore is invariable.

un chapeau **bleu marine**   *une robe* **bleu marine** (navy blue)
un papier **rose foncé** (deep pink) *une* **robe rose clair** (light pink)

Note: *Clair, foncé* and compound colors are invariable.

6.4   Comparing with Adjectives

For comparisons of **equality,** use *aussi* + adjective + *que:*

Françoise est **aussi intelligente que** *son frère.* Frances is as smart as her brother.

*Jeannette est **aussi jolie que** sa soeur.* Jeanette is as pretty as her sister.

*Un chien est **aussi amusant qu'un chat.*** A dog is as much fun as a cat.

6.4.1 Superiority and Inferiority

For comparisons of **superiority** and **inferiority,** regular adjectives add *"plus"* or *"moins:"*

*Ce livre est **plus cher** que l'autre.* This book is more expensive than the other.

*Sa veste est **plus longue** que la mienne.* His jacket is longer than mine.

*As-tu un **plus petit morceau** de gâteau?* Do you have a smaller piece of cake?

*Elle cherche une **plus jolie maison** qui est **moins chère.*** She is looking for a nicer house that's cheaper.

6.4.2 *Bon/Meilleur*

The comparative of *bon* is *meilleur* and of *bonne* is *meilleure.* Just as you don't say "gooder" in English, you don't say it in French!

*Ce **vin** est **meilleur** que le vin suedois.* This wine is better than Swedish wine.

*Je voudrais acheter **une meilleure télévision.*** I'd like to buy a better television.

For a **negative** comparison of *bon:*

*Celui-ci est un mauvais restaurant mais Chez Jean est **pire** (or **plus mauvais**).* This [one] is a bad restaurant but Chez Jean is worse. (You can also use *"moins bon."*)

42

6.4.3 *Petit/Moindre*

"Petit" has an irregular form when used in an abstract sense:

*Cette **loi** est de **moindre importance**.* This law is of lesser importance.

When used in a concrete sense:

*Leur bâteau est **plus petit** que le nôtre.* Their boat is smaller than ours.

6.4.4 Superlatives

Just as in English, the superlative is formed by **adding the definite article to the comparative.**

For adjectives that precede the noun: *le plus, le moins* + adjective + *de* + noun (the most, the least... in the...)

*Il a acheté **la plus belle voiture du village**.* He bought the most beautiful car in the village.
*La **plus petite fille de l'école** va chanter.* The smallest girl in the school is going to sing.
*Voilà **le moins bon vin de la saison**.* There's the worst wine of the season.
*Il choisit **les meilleurs desserts** pour la fête.* He's choosing the best desserts for the party.

Adjectives that follow the noun: The superlative is formed by **naming the noun** and **adding the article and the adjective.** Note that there are **two definite articles** in this structure.

*Nous avons vu **le film le plus populaire** de l'année.* We saw the most popular film of the year.
*Quel est **l'étudiant le moins intelligent** du lycée?* Who is the least intelligent student in the high school?
*J'ai rencontré **la femme la plus célèbre** de Washington.* I met the most famous woman in Washington.

43

6.5   Possessive Adjectives

Since all adjectives **agree with the nouns they modify,** possessive adjectives also follow this rule. Unlike English, where the **possessor** determines the number and gender (his car, her uncles), in French the **object possessed** determines the adjective's gender and number.

6.5.1   Masculine

Masculine singular: one owner, one object

mon livre	my book
ton ami	your friend (**You** can be male or female; the **friend** is male.)
son oncle	his or her uncle (Gender of the **possessor** is determined by the **context.**)

Masculine plural: one owner, two or more objects

mes livres	my books
tes amis	your friends
ses oncles	his or her uncles

6.5.2   Feminine

Feminine singular:

ma robe	my dress
ta cousine	your cousin (**You** can be male or female; the **cousin** is female.)
sa maison	his or her house

Feminine plural:

mes robes	my dresses
tes cousines	your female cousins
ses maisons	his or her houses

6.5.3 Plural Owners

Plural owners: one masculine or feminine object

notre père – our father
votre mère – your mother
leur jardin – their garden

Plural owners: two or more masculine or feminine objects

nos voitures – our cars
vos parents – your parents
leurs bateaux – their boats

6.5.4 *Mon, Ton,* and *Son* Before a Feminine Noun

Before a **feminine** noun that has **an initial vowel,** use "*mon,*" "*ton,*" and "*son.*"

Voilà **mon amie** *Laure.* There's my friend Laura.
Elle a oublié **ton adresse.** She forgot your address.
Son enfant *est malade.* Her (Laura's) child is sick.

But:
Voilà **ma bonne amie** *Laure.* Here is my good friend Laura.
Elle ne sait pas **ta nouvelle adresse.** She doesn't know your new
   address.
Sa petite enfant *est malade.* Her small child is sick.

6.6 Demonstrative Adjectives ("this," "these")

As the name indicates, these adjectives indicate which of several
objects or people are being singled out.

Masculine singular: *Ce livre est bon.*
Feminine singular: *Cette jupe me plaît.*
Masculine and **feminine plural:** *Ces hommes, ces femmes sont
   jeunes.*

Note: Before a **masculine singular** noun with an initial vowel, use *"cet"*:

cet arbre; cet homme; cet état; cet article

The **plural** of *cet* is *ces:*

ces arbres; ces articles; etc.

Before a **feminine singular** noun with an initial vowel, use *cette:*

cette industrie; cette école; cette amie

The **plural** of *cette* is *ces:*

ces écoles; ces amies; etc.

Note: You may add *"–ci"* or *"–là"* to the noun to indicate if the object is closer or farther away:

Ce village-ci est plus grand que ce village-là. This town (here) is larger than that one (there).

6.7　Interrogative Adjectives

To ask "which" or "which one" of a group of things, use *"quel," "quelle,"* or *"quels"* and *"quelles."*

Quel jour sommes-nous? What day is it?
Quelle plage préfères-tu? Which beach do you prefer?
Quels amis t'ont téléphoné? Which friends phoned you?
Quelles chansons vont-ils présenter? Which songs will they perform?

Note: *Quel* may also be an exclamation:

Quelle belle femme! What a beautiful woman!
Quels problèmes! What problems!

6.8 Adjectives of Number

Cardinal numbers are invariable, except for *un, vingt,* and *cent,* which under certain conditions **agree with the noun** they modify:

*Il a écrit **quatre-vingts** articles.* He wrote 80 articles. **But:** *Il a écrit **quatre-vingt-trois** articles.*
*Achetez **vingt** assiettes.* Buy 20 plates. **But:** *Achetez **vingt et une** assiettes.*
*Son manteau coûte deux **cents** dollars.* Her coat costs $200. **But** if the number is **more than 200,** there is no agreement: *Cela coûte **deux cent cinq** dollars.*

6.9 *Demi(e)*: Half

*Le train arrivera à **une heure et demie.*** The train will arrive at 1:30. *"Demie"* agrees with *"heure,"* which is feminine.
*Nous déjeunons à **midi et demi.*** We have lunch at 12:30. *"Midi"* is masculine.

Note: When *demi* **precedes** the noun, it is **masculine:**

*Je voudrais bien prendre une **demi-tasse** de café.* I would like a half cup of coffee.

6.10 Indefinite Adjectives

As the name indicates, they describe a generalized and non-specific noun:

Indefinite Adjectives

Masculine	Feminine	Definition, Example
Singular: *tout*	*toute*	All of **one** class of things: *tout le monde; toute la famille; tout le livre* (the entire, or whole book). The verb is **singular.**

Masculine	Feminine	Definition, Example
Plural: *tous*	*toutes*	*Tous mes amis; toutes les chansons.* The verb is **plural.**
plusieurs	*plusieurs*	Several: *plusieurs amis/ amies*
quelque(s)	*quelque(s)*	Some, a few: *quelque temps libre; quelque part; quelques cartes.*
aucun (sing. only)	*aucune*	Not one, no: *aucun cadeau; aucune femme; aucun argent.*
certain(s)	*certaine(s)*	Certain, some: *certaines personnes; certains jours.*
chaque	*chaque*	Each, every: *chaque jour; chaque fois.*
différent(s)	*différente(s)*	Different: *Il y a de différents livres; de différentes femmes.*
n'importe quel(s)	*n'importe quelle(s)*	Any...whatsoever: *Vous trouverez de bons vins dans n'im-porte quelle région de France.*

CHAPTER 7

Pronouns

Pronouns take the place of nouns and have many functions in French. **Personal pronouns** may replace persons or things and act as **subjects, direct** or **indirect objects.**

7.1   Subject Pronouns

Subject pronouns perform the action of the verb.

First Person
Je   I
nous   we (masc. or fem.)

Je fais le travail. I do the work.
Nous l'aimons. We like it.

Second Person
tu   you (masc. or fem., familiar)
vous   you (singular, formal)
vous   you (plural)

Tu danses bien. You dance well.
Vous partez tôt. You're leaving early.

Third Person

il	he, it (masc.)
elle	she, it (fem.)
ils	they (masc. plural or masc. and fem. plural: *Jean et Marie = ils*)
elles	they (fem. plural)

Elle est malade. She's sick.
Ils comprennent tout. They understand everything.

7.2　Direct Object Pronouns

Direct object pronouns **receive** the action of the verb **directly** without any interference from another person or object.

First Person

me	me (masc. or fem.)
nous	us (masc. or fem.)

*Edgar **me** déteste.* Edgar hates me.
*Mon ami **nous** invite.* My friend's inviting us.

Second Person

te	you (masc. or fem., familiar)
vous	you (masc. or fem., singular or plural)

Sam t'aime. Sam loves you.
*Irma **vous** regarde.** Irma's looking at you.

J'écoute la radio. Je l'écoute. I listen to the radio. I listen to it.
J'attends l'autobus. Je l'attends. I'm waiting for the bus. I'm waiting for it.

Third Person

le	him, it (masc.)
la	her, it (fem.)
les	them (masc. or fem. plural)

Je cherche le chat. Je le cherche. * I'm looking for the cat. I'm looking for him.

Il voit la table. Il la voit. He sees the table. He sees it.

Tu fais les exercices. Tu les fais. You're doing the exercises. You're doing them.

* Note: *"Regarder"* (to look at) and *"chercher"* (to look or search for) take a **direct object** in French. Similarly, *"écouter"* (to listen to) and *"attendre"* (to wait for) take **direct objects.**

7.2.1   Position in Sentence

Object pronouns **precede** the verb. Whereas in English, the word order is **subject–verb–object** (I see you), in French, it is **subject–object–verb** *(Je te vois).*

7.3   Indirect Object Pronouns

Indirect object pronouns include the preposition *"à"* (to) in their meaning. Only the third person pronouns change for indirect objects; *me, te, nous, vous* appear in the same forms for **direct and indirect** objects.

Gaston m'a parlé. Gaston spoke to me.

Il va t'écrire. He'll write to you.

Marie nous a envoyé des fleurs. Marie sent us flowers.

Paul veut lui téléphoner. Paul wants to phone her.

Note: *"Téléphoner à quelqu'un"* takes an **indirect object** in French.

Hint: Just as the word "indirect" is longer than the word "direct," third person indirect object pronouns are **longer** than direct object pronouns:

Direct Object Pronouns
Third person: *le, la, les*

Indirect Object Pronouns

Third person: *lui* – to him, to her; *leur** – to them (masc. or fem.)

* Note: **Leur** (to him, to her) is invariable. Do not confuse it with the possessive adjective *"leur" mère* (their mother) or *"leurs" amis* (their friends).

7.3.1   Position of Indirect Object Pronouns

As with direct object pronouns, indirect object pronouns **precede** the verb:

> *Nous **lui** envoyons une lettre.* We're sending him (or her) a letter.
> *Nancy répond à ses cousins. Elle **leur** répond.* Nancy answers her cousins. She answers them.

Note: *"Répondre à"* takes an **indirect object.**

7.4   With Two Verbs Together

With two verbs together, place the object pronoun **before the infinitive:**

> *Il veut faire ce dîner. Il veut **le** faire.* He wants to make dinner. He wants to make it.
> *Margot va **lui** écrire.* Margot will write to him.

7.5   With Two Object Pronouns Together

With two object pronouns together, the order is **numerical** for the **first** and **second persons:**

> *Il me donne le livre.* (*"me"* = 1st person; *"le"* = 3rd person. 1st before 3rd: *Il **me le** donne.)*

> *Paul vous envoie vos cadeaux. Paul **vous les** envoie.* (2nd person before 3rd person.)

me, nous before *le, la, les*
te, vous before *le, la, les*

With two third person pronouns together, the order is **alphabetical:**

*Bill vend sa voiture à Mireille. Il **la lui** vend.*
*Elle offre ces photos à ses parents. Elle **les leur** offre.*

le, la, les before *lui, leur*

7.6   *Y* and *en; penser à; parler de*

These two pronouns replace places, things, ideas, expressions, **rather than people.**

"*Y*" replaces expressions which require the preposition "*à*" or any other preposition of place, other than "*de*":

*Il va à l'aeroport. Il **y** va.* He's going to the airport. He's going there.
*Les fleurs sont **sur la table**. Elles **y** sont.* The flowers are on the table. They're on it.
*Nous avons mis son argent **dans le tiroir**. Nous **y** avons mis son argent.* We put his money in the drawer. We put his money there.
*Elle a répondu **à ta question**. Elle **y** a répondu.* She answered your question. She answered it.
*Les bons citoyens obéissent **aux lois**. Ils **y** obéissent.* Good citizens obey the laws. They obey them.

Note: for the verb "*penser*":

Penser à + a thing = to think about something:

*Il pense à son voyage. Il **y** pense.* He thinks about his trip. He's thinking about it.

Note: ***Penser à*** + a person = disjunctive pronoun (see below):

*Je pense à mon père. Je pense à **lui**.* I think about my father. I'm
  thinking about him.

En replaces expressions with ***de,*** including quantities:

*As-tu beaucoup **de temps libre**? Non, je **n'en ai pas** beaucoup.*
  Do you have much free time? I don't have much.
*Ma soeur revient **de Paris**. Elle **en** revient.* My sister's returning
  from Paris. She's returning from there.
*A-t-il parlé **de ses aventures?** Oui, il **en** a parlé.* Did he speak
  about his adventures? Yes, he spoke about them.
***Combien de** cousins avez-vous? J'**en** ai cinq.* How many cous-
  ins do you have? I have five (of them).
*Il parle souvent **de ses problèmes**. Il **en** parle souvent.* He often
  talks about his problems. He often talks about them.

Note: The verb *"**parler**"* + *de* + an idea, place or thing = *"**en**":*

*Sam parle de son travail. Il **en** parle.* Sam talks about his work.
  He talks about it.

But: ***parler de*** + a person = a disjunctive pronoun:

*Sam **parle de ses parents**. Il parle d'**eux**.* Sam is talking about
  his parents. He's talking about them.

Note: ***parler à*** + a person = indirect object pronoun:

*Sam **parle à sa petite amie**. Il **lui** parle.* Sam is talking to his
girlfriend. He's talking **to** her.

Résumé:
1. Use *"**y**"* to replace expressions with *"**à**"* and other prepositions (besides *"**de**"*).
2. Use *"**en**"* to replace expressions with *"**de**."*
3. The verbs *"**penser**"* and *"**parler**"* make a distinction between
   pronouns which replace things or people.

a. *Penser à* + a thing = *"y"*
b. *Penser à* + a person = disjunctive pronoun (*à moi, à lui,* etc.)
c. *Penser de:* This form is used only **in a question** seeking an **opinion.** *Que penses-tu de mon chapeau? Qu'en penses-tu?* Answer: *Je pense qu'il est chic.*
d. *Penser de* + a person = disjunctive pronoun. *Que penses-tu de Jean? Que penses-tu de lui?* Answer: *Je pense qu'il est gentil.*

Word order with *"y"* **and** *"en"*: These two pronouns come after direct and indirect object pronouns; *"y"* precedes *"en."*

Je mets les stylos dans la boîte. Je les y mets. I put them there.
Tu as donné de l'argent à Pierre. Tu lui en as donné. You gave him some.

Note: There is never any agreement with *en* in the *passé composé.*

Nous leur avons envoyé des fleurs. Nous leur en avons envoyé. We've sent them some (flowers).

Hint: Remember, the expression *"Il y en a,"* which answers the question *"Y a-t-il (des roses sur la table)?"* —*Oui, il y en a.*

7.7 Interrogative Sentences with Pronouns

As with declarative sentences, pronouns **precede the verb** in **interrogative** sentences:

Avons-nous assez d'argent? En avons-nous assez?* Do we have enough money?
Est-ce que tu connais Marcie? Est-ce que tu la connais? Do you know her?
Ont-ils pris mon stylo? L'ont-ils pris? Did they take it?
Pierre est-il à New York maintenant? Y est-il? Is he there?

* Note: The **adverb** *"assez"* is repeated.

55

7.8   Disjunctive Pronouns

Disjunctive pronouns are **not joined** to the verb, as are those discussed so far. Their forms are: *moi, toi, lui, elle, nous vous, eux, elles.* Their principal uses are:

   a.   After a preposition: *Je vais chez toi. Le livre est devant lui.*
   b.   After *"c'est"*: *Qui parle? C'est elle. C'est lui.*
   c.   With a double subject: *Simon et moi, nous allons à Paris.*
   d.   With *"parler de* + a person." *Je parle de mes amis. Je parle d'eux.*
   e.   With *"penser à* + a person"* and *"penser de* + a person."*
   f.   To emphasize a strong statement: *Moi, j'ai dit cela?* I said that?
   g.   To compare and contrast two elements: *Paul, lui est riche mais Marie, elle est pauvre.*

7.9   Relative Pronouns

Relative pronouns link or relate two ideas or two clauses. They must have an **antecedent** (a noun or pronoun which comes before the pronoun and to which it refers).

7.9.1   Simple Relative Pronouns

Simple relative pronoun forms: *qui* (subject), *que* (object), and *où* (for places and time).

Nous regardons l'homme qui danse si bien. We're watching the man who dances so well. *Qui* links the two ideas and is the **subject** of the verb *"danse."* Antecedent: *l'homme.*
Le livre que tu cherchais as disparu. The book you were looking for has disappeared. *Que* is the **object** of the verb *"chercher."* Antecedent: *le livre.*
Voilà le café où Bill travaille. There's the cafe where Bill works. *Où* designates **"the place where."** Antecedent: *le café.*
Minuit est l'heure où nous nous couchons. Midnight is the time (when) we go to bed. Antecedent: *l'heure.*

Hint: To differentiate **subject** from **object,** remember that *qui* always **precedes the verb directly;** *que* always has **another subject before the verb.**

7.9.2   *Ce qui, ce que*

Ce qui, ce que are used in sentences where there is **no antecedent.** *"Ce"* = "the thing that" or "what":

Tu ne sais pas ce qui est bon. You don't know what's good.
Je comprends ce que Sam dit. I understand what Sam is saying.

7.9.3   *Lequel, laquelle, lesquels, lesquelles*

Lequel, laquelle, lesquels, and *lesquelles* are relative pronouns that are used **after prepositions** to replace people or things. The pronoun agrees with its **antecedent:**

C'est le stylo avec lequel le Président a signé la loi. That's the
pen with which the President signed the law.
Où est la maison dans laquelle tu habitais? Where's the house
in which you used to live?
Voici les gens sans lesquels nous ne pouvons pas partir. Here are
the people without whom we can't leave.
Connaissez-vous les femmes pour lesquelles il a écrit ses poèmes?
Do you know the women for whom he wrote his poems?
Sara est la femme de laquelle je t'ai parlé. Sara is the woman
about whom I spoke to you.
Est-ce François l'homme auquel tu as vendu ton vélo? Is Francis
the fellow to whom you sold your bike?

Note: After a preposition, you may use *lequel* (or *auquel, duquel, de laquelle, desquels, desquelles)* or *qui* for **people** but you must only use *lequel* for things.

Exception: After *"parmi"* (among), use *lequel* for people:

Voilà des étudiants parmi lesquels se trouve ta cousine. There
are some students, among whom is your cousin.

7.9.4 *Dont*

Dont is often used instead of *duquel, de laquelle,* etc. (of which, of whom or whose) to replace people or things:

> *La personne dont vous parlez n'est plus en ville.* The person of whom you're speaking is not in town.
> *Yves, dont le frère est Paul, comprend la situation.* Yves, whose brother is Paul, understands the situation.

Ce dont is used when there is **no antecedent** (the thing about which, of which). Remember that there is always a *"de"* that is being replaced when you use *"dont"*:

> *Je ne comprends pas ce dont vous avez besoin.* [*avoir besoin + de* something]. I don't understand what you need.
> *Ce dont ils parlent me fait peur.* [*parler + de* something]. What they're talking about frightens me.

7.10 Possessive Pronouns

Possessive pronouns take the place of nouns and agree with them in number and gender.

7.10.1 Forms of Possessive Pronouns

Remember that the pronoun agrees with the object possessed, **not with the gender of the possessor.**

First person	Second Person	Third Person
le mien – mine, m. sing.	*le tien* – yours	*le sien* – his, hers, m. sing.
les miens –mine, m. pl.	*les tiens* – yours	*les siens* – his, hers
le nôtre – ours, m.s.	*le vôtre* – yours	*le leur* – theirs
la mienne– mine, f. sing.	*la tienne* – yours, f. sing.	*la sienne* – his, hers, f. sing.
les miennes – mine, f. pl.	*les tiennes* – yours, f. pl.	*les siennes* – his, hers, f. pl.
les nôtres – ours, m. or f. pl.	*les vôtres* – yours, pl.	*les leurs* – theirs, m. or f. pl.

58

*Où sont tes amis? **Les miens** sont ici.* Where are your friends?
Mine are here.

*Ta robe est jolie. **La sienne** est laide.* Your dress is pretty. Hers is
ugly.

*Nos oncles sont là. **Les leurs** sont partis.* Our uncles are here.
Theirs left.

CHAPTER 8

Verbs

Verbs are the heart of the sentence and **express an action or a state of being, mental or physical.** There are several **moods** of verbs (means of communication) and each mood contains **tenses** (time of the action). *L'indicatif, l'impératif, le conditionnel,* and *le subjontif* are the principal moods we will discuss.

8.1   *L'indicatif*

L'indicatif (the indicative) indicates or relates information in either declarative or interrogative sentences. It has three main conjugations: *–er, –ir,* or *–re* verbs. The *infinitif* (the "to" form) is made up of **a stem + an ending.**

8.1.1   Regular *–er* verbs

Regular *–er* verbs: *chanter, danser, manger, donner, parler,* etc.
Note: The great majority of French verbs are of this conjugation.

Present tense of *chanter* (to sing). *Chant* = stem (or radical) + *er* = ending.

Present participle = *chantant* (singing)

je chante	*nous chantons*
(I sing, I am singing, I do sing)	
tu chantes	*vous chantez*
il (elle, on) chante	*ils (elles) chantent*

60

8.1.2   –ir verbs

There are two classes of *–ir* verbs, those that add *"-iss-"* to the plural forms *(finir, choisir, réussir, fleurir, brunir)* and those that do not *(dormir, sortir, partir)*. The **present participles** of *finir = finissant* (finishing) and *dormir = dormant* (sleeping) also reflect these differences.

Finir:

je finis	*nous finissons*
tu finis	*vous finissez*
il finit	*ils finissent*

Dormir:

je dors	*nous dormons*
tu dors	*vous dormez*
il (elle) dort	*ils (elles) dorment*

8.1.3   Regular –re verbs

Regular verbs ending in *–re (vendre, rendre, attendre, descendre):*

Attendre (to wait for)   **present participle:** *attendant*

j'attends	*nous attendons*
tu attends	*vous attendez*
il (elle) attend	*ils (elles) attendent*

8.1.4   Verbs ending in –oir

Verbs ending in *–oir (voir, recevoir, pouvoir, vouloir, devoir,* etc.) are irregular but commonly follow a pattern: 1st, 2nd, 3rd persons singular and 3rd person plural are **similar:**

Voir (to see)   **present participle:** *voyant*

je vois	*nous voyons*
tu vois	*vous voyez*
il (elle) voit	*ils (elles) voient*

Vouloir (to want, to wish)   **present participle:** *voulant*
   je veux   *nous voulons*
   tu veux   *vous voulez*
   il (elle) veut   *ils (elles) veulent*

Recevoir (to receive)   **present participle:** *recevant*
   je reçois   *nous recevons*
   tu reçois   *vous recevez*
   il (elle) reçoit   *ils (elles) reçoivent*

Note: No cedilla is used under the "c" when it is before "e."

8.1.5   Spelling Changes in *–er* Verbs

Some otherwise regular *–er* verbs have **spelling changes** in the *"nous"* and *"vous"* forms:

appeler:	*j'appelle*	*nous appelons*	*vous appelez*
jeter:	*je jette*	*nous jetons*	*vous jetez*
acheter:	*j'achète*	*nous achetons*	*vous achetez*
espérer:	*j'espère*	*nous espérons*	*vous espérez*
préférer:	*je préfère*	*nous préférons*	*vous préférez*
	ils (elles) préfèrent		

8.1.6   Common Irregular Verbs

Common irregular verbs (with present participle)

Être (étant)
je suis	*nous sommes*
tu es	*vous êtes*
il (elle) est	*ils (elles) sont*

Avoir (ayant)
j'ai	*nous avons*
tu as	*vous avez*
il (elle) a	*ils (elles) ont*

Faire (faisant)
je fais	*nous faisons*
tu fais	*vous faites*
il (elle) fait	*ils (elles) font*

Aller (allant)
je vais	*nous allons*
tu vas	*vous allez*
il (elle) va	*ils (elles) vont*

Note: *ils **ont** (avoir); ils **sont** (être); ils **font** (faire); ils **vont** (aller)*

Venir (venant)
je viens   nous venons
tu viens   vous venez
il (elle) vient   ils (elles) viennent

Pouvoir (pouvant)
je peux   nous pouvons
tu peux   vous pouvez
il (elle) peut   ils (elles) peuvent

Dire (disant)
je dis   nous disons
tu dis   vous dites
il (elle) dit   ils (elles) disent

Envoyer (envoyant)
j'envoie   nous envoyons
tu envoies   vous envoyez
il (elle) envoie   ils (elles) envoient

Prendre (prenant)
je prends   nous prenons
tu prends   vous prenez
il (elle) prend   ils (elles) prennent

Écrire (écrivant)
j'écris   nous écrivons
tu écris   vous écrivez
il (elle) écrit   ils (elles) écrivent

Craindre (craignant)
je crains   nous craignons
tu crains   vous craignez
il (elle) craint   ils (elles) craignent

Savoir (sachant)
je sais   nous savons
tu sais   vous savez
il (elle) sait   ils (elles) savent

Boire (buvant)
je bois   nous buvons
tu bois   vous buvez
il (elle) boit   ils (elles) boivent

Lire (lisant)
je lis   nous lisons
tu lis   vous lisez
il (elle) lit   ils (elles) lisent

8.1.7   Interrogative Sentences

Questions are usually formed most simply by adding *"Est ce-que?"* to a declarative sentence:

Est-ce que Robert lit beaucoup? Does Robert read a lot?
Est-ce que tu veux aller avec nous? Do you want to go with us?
Est-ce que l'enfant sait lire? Does the child know how to read?

Questions are also formed by **inversion**, i.e., placing the verb **before** the **subject**:

Buvez-vous trop de café? Do you drink too much coffee?
Avons-nous les billets? Do we have the tickets?
Travailles-tu maintenant? Are you working now?

Note: When the subject is in the third person, **name the subject** and **then invert the verb-pronoun** for a question:

Ces femmes ont-elles assez d'argent? Do these women have enough money?
La guerre est-elle nécessaire? Is war necessary?
Sylvie prépare-t-elle un grand dîner? Is Sylvia making a big dinner?

8.2 *L'impératif*

L'impératif, another **mood**, expresses **commands** or **orders**.
Formation: use the present form of *tu, nous,* and *vous* **without the subject pronoun.**

8.2.1 Affirmative Commands

Réponds, Jim! Answer, Jim!
Choisis une pomme! Take an apple!
Rends mon argent! Give back my money!
Marie, regarde la lune! Mary, look at the moon!
Donne le stylo à ton papa! Give your dad the pen!
Va avec Sam! Go with Sam!

Note: There is no "s" in the *"tu"* form of *–er* verbs.

Marchons vite! Let's walk fast!
Écrivons la lettre! Let's write the letter!
Fermez la porte! Close the door!
Finissez le vin! Finish the wine!
Prenez votre manteau! Take your coat!

8.2.2 Negative Commands

For **negative commands,** place *ne* in front of the verb and *pas* after it:

Ne réponds pas! Don't answer!
Ne rends pas mon argent! Don't give back my money!
Ne fermez pas la porte! Don't close the door!
Ne prenez pas votre manteau! Don't take your coat!

8.2.3 Irregular Imperatives

There are only **three irregular imperative forms:**

Avoir: aie, ayons, ayez
Etre: sois, soyons, soyez
Savoir: sache, sachons, sachez

N'aie pas peur! Don't be afraid!
Soyez calme! Be calm!
Sachons la vérité! Let's learn the truth!

8.2.4 Imperative + Pronoun

Imperative + pronoun: With **affirmative** commands, use *le, la, les, nous* for **direct objects** and *moi, nous, lui, leur* for **indirect objects.** Place pronouns **after the verb:**

Regarde-le! Look at it!
Mange-les! Eat them!
Fais-le! Do it!
Écrivez-moi! Write to me!
Parlons-lui! Let's speak to him (her)!

8.2.5 With Negative Commands

With negative commands, place the pronoun **before the verb:**

Ne le regarde pas! Don't look at it!
Ne les mange pas! Don't eat it!

*Ne **le** fais pas!* Don't do it!
*Ne **m'**écrivez pas!* Don't write to me!
*Ne **lui** parlons pas!* Don't talk to him.

8.2.6   With Two Pronouns

With two pronouns place **people** at the end of the sentence for emphasis in **affirmative commands.** Use regular pronoun order in **negative commands:**

*Donne-le-**moi**!* Give it to me! **But:** *Ne **me** le donne pas!*
*Envoyez-les-**nous**!* Send them to us! **But:** *Ne **nous** les envoyez pas!*
*Ecrivez-la-**leur**!* Write it to them! **But:** *Ne **la leur** écrivez pas!*

8.2.7   *Y* and *en*

Y and *en* follow the personal pronouns. Note these details:

*Vas-**y**!* Go to it! (Add "s" before the vowel.) **But:** *N'**y** va pas!*
*Mettez-les-**y**!* Put them there! *Ne les **y** mettez pas!*
*Manges-**en**!* Eat some of it! (Add "s" before the vowel.) *N'**en** mange pas!*
*Parlez-**lui-en**!* Speak to him about it! *Ne **lui en** parlez pas!*
*Donne-**m'en**!* Give me some! *Ne **m'en** donne pas!*

8.3   *Le passé composé*

Le passé composé is in the indicative mood. The name of this tense (compound past) illustrates the fact that it is made up of **more than one part.** (A "simple" verb has only one component.) There are **two parts** to the passé composé: an **auxiliary verb** *(avoir* or *être)* and a **past participle,** which is a verbal, **not a verb,** and **can never stand alone as a verb.**

8.3.1   Formation

–er **verbs:** To form the past participle, drop the *–er* of the infinitive and add *"é."*

donner: to give

j'ai donné	*nous avons donné*
tu as donné	*vous avez donné*
il (elle) a donné	*ils (elles) ont donné*

Note: ***Avoir*** is conjugated; the participle is invariable.

–ir verbs: To form the past participle, drop the "r" of the infinitive to form the participle.

choisir: to choose

j'ai choisi	*nous avons choisi*
tu as choisi	*vous avez choisi*
il (elle) a choisi	*ils (elles) ont choisi*

–re verbs: To form the past participle, drop the "–re" and add "u" to the stem.

vendre: to sell

j'ai vendu	*nous avons vendu*
tu as vendu	*vous avez vendu*
il (elle) a vendu	*ils (elles) ont vendu*

8.3.2 Past Participles of Irregular Verbs

The above patterns apply to all **regular** verbs; for **irregular** verbs, participles must be learned separately. Here are some common examples:

avoir: j'ai eu	*être: j'ai été*	*écrire: j'ai écrit*
courir: j'ai couru	*boire: j'ai bu*	*croire: j'ai cru*
dire: j'ai dit	*prendre: j'ai pris*	*ouvrir: j'ai ouvert*
tenir: j'ai tenu	*faire: j'ai fait*	*lire: j'ai lu*
voir: j'ai vu	*savoir: j'ai su*	*vouloir: j'ai voulu*
pouvoir: j'ai pu	*mettre: j'ai mis*	*vivre: j'ai vécu*
recevoir: j'ai reçu	*plaire: j'ai plu*	

8.3.3 *L'Accord* (Agreement)

In the *passé composé* with the auxiliary *avoir,* if there is a **direct object** (noun or pronoun) that **precedes** the **verb** the participle must "agree" with the direct object in gender and number (for feminine and plural). Masculine singular objects that precede the verb do not affect the participle.

> *Pierre a pris ces chemises.* *("Chemises"* is the direct object of *"a pris.") Il les a prises.* *("Les"* is the feminine plural direct object that precedes the verb; therefore, you add "es" to the participle *"pris.")*
>
> *Nous avons vendu la voiture. Nous l'avons vendue.* *("Voiture"* is feminine singular, *"l"* replaces *"voiture;"* *"vendu"* must agree; therefore, you add an "e.")

Note: When the **direct object follows the verb** *("ces chemises," "la voiture"),* the participle is **invariable.**

> *As-tu rencontré Marie? L'as-tu rencontrée?* Did you meet Marie? Did you meet her?

ATTENTION:
Nous avons téléphoné à nos amis. Nous leur avons téléphoné. (Agreement is made **only** with the preceding **direct object,** not the **indirect object.)**

8.3.4 *Passé composé* with *être*

There are about 20 verbs which form the *passé composé* with *être,* rather than with *avoir.* (Cf., "Joy to the World/The Lord **is** come" in Old English.) These verbs deal with the comings and goings, with the extremities of life.

aller – to go	*parvenir* – to reach or achieve
arriver – to arrive	*passer* – to pass, drop by, spend time
descendre – to come down	*rentrer* – to come or go home
devenir – to become	*rester* – to stay, remain

entrer – to enter	*retourner* – to return
monter – to go up, climb	*revenir* – to come back, return
mourir – to die	*sortir* – to go out
naître – to be born	*tomber* – to fall
partir – to leave, depart	*venir* – to come

8.3.5 Agreement with *être*

The past participle used with *être* must agree in number and gender with the subject.

*Elles **sont nées** à Paris.* They (fem. pl.) were born in Paris.
*Son amie **est morte** hier.* His friend (fem.) died yesterday.
*Nous **sommes arrivés** en retard.* We arrived late.
*Mathilde **est tombée** de son lit.* Matilda fell from her bed.

8.3.6 Transitive and Intransitive Verbs

Rentrer, sortir, monter, descendre, passer may be used **transitively** (with a direct object) or **intransitively** (with no object.) When they are **transitive verbs,** they take *avoir:*

J'ai rentré *la voiture.* I brought the car inside.
*Marie **a monté** la rue Diderot.* Marie went up Diderot Street.
*Bill **a descendu** les valises.* Bill brought the suitcases down.
*Yvette **m'a passé** le pain.* Yvette passed me the bread.

Note: Rules of agreement for *avoir* apply to these five verbs when they are **transitive:** The participle agrees with the preceding **direct object.**

*Je l'ai **rentrée**.* I brought it (the car) in.
*Marie l'a **montée**.* Marie went up it (the street).
*Bill les a **descendues**.* Bill brought them (the suitcases) down.

8.3.7 Interrogative in the *Passé Composé*

With *est-ce que:*
*Est-ce que Jacques **a téléphoné**? **Est-il passé** ce matin?* Did Jack

call? Did he come by this morning?

With **inversion:**

Jacques a-t-il téléphoné? (Note: In conversation, the structure *"Jacques a téléphoné?"* is more common.)
Où êtes-vous allés, mes amis? Where did you go, my friends?
Tes parents sont-ils partis? Did your folks leave?

8.3.8 Negative

Since all negatives have two parts *(ne...pas, ne...jamais, ne...pas encore*, etc.), place *ne* before the **verb** *(avoir* or *être)* and *pas, plus*, etc. after the verb.

Il n'a pas vu ton chien. He didn't see your dog.
Nous n'avons plus parlé de lui. We didn't speak of him any longer.
Jeanne n'est jamais allée à Nîmes. Jeannie never went to Nîmes.
Pourquoi n'ont-ils pas encore écrit? Why haven't they written yet?

Negative interrogative + object pronoun with *avoir:* (With *être,* the object pronoun is used only in pronominal verb constructions — see below.)

A-t-elle mis la robe? Ne l'a-t-elle pas mise? Did she wear the dress? Didn't she wear it?
Les Duval n'ont-ils pas acheté cette maison? Ne l'ont-ils pas achetée? Didn't the Duvals buy that house? Didn't they buy it?

8.4 *L'imparfait*

The term **"imperfect"** signifies **"not perfected** or **finished"** and this attribute distinguishes it from the *passé composé.* Unlike the *passé composé,* it is a simple form (with no auxiliary).

8.4.1 Formation

Take the *"nous"* form of the present tense, remove the ending *"ons."* To the remaining stem, add: *–ais, –ais, –ait, –ions, –iez, –aient.* **Exception:** *j'étais.*

Je dansais. I danced, I used to dance, I was dancing.

Donner: *je donnais*	**Finir:** *je finissais*
Écrire: *j'écrivais*	**Étudier:** *j'étudiais, nous étudiions*
Manger: *je mangeais*	**Commencer:** *je commençais*
Préfèrer: *je préférais*	**Appeler:** *j'appelais*

8.4.2 Usage

Unlike the *passé composé,* which denotes **an action completed within a specified or implied time frame,** the imperfect is a tense of **description, condition, repetition,** or **habitual action.** This time frame can also be prolonged when using the *imparfait* for a repeated, habitual or routine action in the past. For example: *Tous les matins je me promenais au bord de la mer.* Every morning I used to (I would) go for a walk by the ocean.

Quand j'étais jeune, je faisais beaucoup de sport. [General description of habitual, repeated action.] When I was young, I played a lot of sports.

Puisque Marc avait mal au dos, il ne pouvait pas marcher vite. [Description of physical/mental condition.] Since Marc had a backache, he couldn't walk fast.

Le ciel était bleu, le vent touchait légèrement le bout des fleurs, qui semblaient heureuses. Il faisait très beau et nous avions envie de rester au jardin mais il fallait rentrer dans la maison. The sky was blue, the wind lightly touched the edges of the flowers, which seemed to be happy. It was a beautiful day and we felt like staying in the garden, but we had to go inside the house. [As you can see, an entire passage may be expressed in the imperfect, if it involves description of the weather, the décor, mental and/or physical conditions, i.e., "how things were."]

8.4.3 *Quand*

Two **simultaneous actions** that took place in the past may be expressed by the imperfect using *quand*.

> *Quand nous parlions, elle regardait la télé.* When we were speaking, she was watching TV.
> *Claude avait cinq ans quand son père travaillait à Nice.* Claude was five years old when her father was working in Nice.
> *Quand tu entrais, nous sortions.* When you were coming in, we were going out.

Attention:
Robert ne savait pas quand son cousin allait revenir. Robert didn't know when his cousin was going to return.

Note: *"Aller"* is **always** used in the **imperfect** as an auxiliary to express the future in the past ("was going to do something").

8.4.4 *L'imparfait* versus *le passé composé*

Although theoretically any verb may be used in any tense, some verbs are used **almost exclusively** in the **imperfect** because of their meaning, e.g., *être, avoir, pouvoir, vouloir, savoir, aimer, détester, préférer,* etc., which describe conditions, states of mind, or emotions.

Under certain circumstances, these verbs may be used in the *passé composé* in order to isolate a particular moment or an extraordinary situation or event.

> *Ce matin elle a eu mal à la tête à cause de son accident hier.* This morning she had a headache because of her accident yesterday. [The headache is gone now.]

72

*Le garçon regardait attentivement le film et tout à coup il **a pu** comprendre l'histoire.* The boy watched the movie carefully and all at once he could understand the story. [He succeeded in grasping it.]

*Le chat a vu le chien et soudain il **a voulu** courir.* The cat saw the dog and suddenly he tried to run. [The sense of *"vouloir"* is "to try" in this case.]

Hint: Key words like ***tout à coup, soudain, immédiatement*** often indicate the extraordinary circumstances that call for the use of the *passé composé* for these verbs.

Remember that the *passé composé* stands for an **action completed** in a **specified** or **implied time.** The *imparfait* is ongoing and has **no indicated beginning or end.**

Compare:

*Nous **écrivions** une carte postale quand le train **est arrivé**.* We were writing a post card when the train arrived. [*Passé composé* interrupts the ongoing action of the imperfect.]

*Sophie **a ouvert** la boîte et **a ri** de plaisir.* Sophie opened the box and laughed with pleasure. [Two actions in the *passé composé*; one inspires the other.]

*Sam **était** fatigué et **ne voulait pas** manger.* Sam was tired and didn't want to eat. [Two descriptive actions; both imperfect.]

8.5   Le plus-que-parfait

The *pluperfect* denotes something further away in the past. It is a compound tense that is used to **compare two past actions.** It may be used with the *passé composé* or the imperfect.

8.5.1   Formation

The imperfect form of *avoir* or *être* is used as an **auxiliary** with the **past participle.** The same rules of **agreement** that apply to the *passé composé* govern the *plus-que-parfait*.

*Hier **j'ai reçu** la lettre que Jean **avait envoyée** il y a trois semaines.*

73

Yesterday I received the letter that John (had) sent three weeks ago. [The action of sending the letter precedes its receipt. Both actions are in the past.]

*Gigi **était déjà arrivée** quand **nous avons téléphoné**.* Gigi had already arrived when we phoned.

*Philippe **oubliait** toujours le nom des gens qu'il **avait rencontrés**.* Philip always used to forget the names of people he (had) met.

8.6 Le futur proche

Le futur proche (the near future) is expressed by using *"aller"* in the present tense as an **auxiliary + the infinitive.**

*Nous **allons voir** le nouvel ami de Laure ce soir.* We're going to see Laura's new friend this evening.

***Vas-tu payer** cette facture?* Are you going to pay this bill?

*L'année prochaine **ils ne vont pas visiter** le Midi.* Next year they're not going to visit the south of France.

8.7 Le futur

This tense is a simple tense whose formation is based on the **infinitive + forms of *"avoir."***

8.7.1 Formation of Future Tense for Regular Verbs

je parlerai	*je finirai*	*je vendrai*
tu parleras	*tu finiras*	*tu vendras*
il parlera	*il finira*	*il vendra*
elle parlera	*elle finira*	*elle vendra*
nous parlerons	*nous finirons*	*nous vendrons*
vous parlerez	*vous finirez*	*vous vendrez*
ils parleront	*ils finiront*	*ils vendront*
elles parleront	*elles finiront*	*elles vendront*

8.7.2 Common Irregular Verbs

Stems change; endings do not.

*avoir: j'**aur**ai*	*être: je **ser**ai*	*faire: je **fer**ai*
*aller: j'**ir**ai*	*dire: je **dir**ai*	*venir: je **viendr**ai*
*courir: je **courr**ai*	*pouvoir: je **pourr**ai*	*vouloir: je **voudr**ai*
*écrire: j'**écrir**ai*	*essayer: j'**essaier**ai*	*voir: je **verr**ai*

*Quand **je serai** à Paris, **j'irai** le voir.* When I'm in Paris, I'll go see him.

*Je ne sais pas quand elle **partira**.* I don't know when she's leaving.

Note: When *"quand"* is followed by a **future action,** the verb must be in the **future,** even though in English we often translate it in the present.

8.7.3 Expressing Probability

The future can be used to express **probability:**

*Il est minuit, Paul **sera** déjà endormi.* It's midnight; Paul is probably asleep already.

*Christine **aura** reçu mon cadeau.* Christine has probably received my present.

8.8 Le conditionnel

The conditional is a **mood** (with a present and past tense) that is always based on a **hypothetical situation** ("if" certain circumstances occur, then...). The "if" may be expressed or implied.

8.8.1 Formation

Like the future, the conditional uses the **infinitive** as its stem; the imperfect forms of *"avoir"* are its endings. Irregular verbs use the forms of the future as the stem.

je parlerais	*je finirais*	*je vendrais*
nous parlerions	*nous finirions*	*nous vendrions*
ils parleraient	*ils finiraient*	*ils vendraient*

Hint: There is always an "r" in the conditional to differentiate it from the imperfect, which has the same endings.

Imperfect	Conditional	Imperfect	Conditional
je dansais	*je danserais*	*je voulais*	*je voudrais*
je venais	*je viendrais*	*je finissais*	*je finirais*
j'étais	*je serais*	*j'avais*	*j'aurais*
je faisais	*je ferais*	*je voyais*	*je verrais*
je finissais	*je finirais*	*je pouvais*	*je pourrais*

*Sans son aide, nous ne **saurions** pas utiliser cette machine.* Without his help, we wouldn't know how to use this machine.

*Pauline **serait** ravie de recevoir ce livre.* Pauline would be delighted to receive this book.

*Je **viendrais** te parler ce soir.* I'd come to talk to you tonight.

*Daniel **voudrait** du poisson et de la salade.* Daniel would like some fish and salad. [The conditional of *"vouloir"* is used for politeness instead of the present of the indicative *"je veux."*]

8.8.2   The Past Conditional

The past conditional is further away in possibility and time, and often expresses regret.

Formation: The conditional of *"avoir"* or *"être"* + **past participle.**

*J'**aurais voulu** le voir.* I would have liked to see him.

*Elle **serait allée** avec toi.* She would have gone with you.

*Nous **ne** leur **aurions pas raconté** cette histoire.* We wouldn't have told them that story.

76

8.8.3 The Future and Conditional with "if" Clauses

If...	Result...
Present: *Si j'ai le temps*	Future: *j'irai chez lui.*
Imperfect: *Si j'avais le temps*	Conditional: *j'irais chez lui.*
Pluperfect: *Si j'avais eu le temps*	Past Conditional: *je serais allé*

These structures correspond to English: If I **have** the time, **I'll do** it; If I **had** the time, I **would do** it; If I **had had** the time, I **would have done** it.

8.9 *L'infinitif*

When two verbs are used together, the **second verb** is always in the **infinitive.** The following verbs are followed **directly** by the infinitive with **no preposition:**

*Nous **aimons** danser.* We like to dance.
*Ils ne **savent** pas lire.* They don't know how to read.
*Margot **déteste** travailler.* Margot hates to work.
*Cet homme **adore** manger.* This man loves to eat.

8.9.1 As a Noun

The infinitive may also be used as a noun, as the subject or object of the sentence or as the object of a preposition:

***Dormir** bien est très important.* Sleeping well is very important.
*Je n'aime pas **dire** "adieu."* I don't like to say "goodbye."

8.9.2 *L'infinitif passé*

L'infinitif passé uses ***"avoir"*** or ***"être"*** as the **auxiliary + the past participle** (*après avoir vu; après être venu*)to express "after having done something." ***"Avant de"*** + the **infinitive** (*avant de voir; avant de venir*) is used for "before doing something."

***Avant de faire** son lit, Marie a cherché des draps.* Before making her bed, Mary looked for some sheets.

*Jacques prépare son dîner **après avoir étudié.*** Jack makes his
dinner after having studied.
*Elle nous a vus **après être rentrée.*** After coming home, she saw
us.
***Après être tombée**, Suzy a ri.* After falling down, Susie laughed.
*Il nous écrira **avant de partir.*** He'll write to us before he leaves.

Note: **One subject** performs **both actions**. The participle agrees
with the **subject** with *"être"* and with the **preceding direct object**
with *"avoir."* The verb in the second action may be in the present,
past, or future tense.

8.10 *Le participe présent*

The present participle is formed by adding **"–ant"** to the stem of
the **"nous"** form of the present:

parlant, finissant, rompant. **Exceptions:** *étant, ayant, sachant.*

8.10.1 As an Adjective

The present participle may act as an **adjective:**

***Pensant** que son chien était perdu, il a commencé à pleurer.*
Thinking his dog was lost, he cried.
*"L'homme est un roseau **pensant.**" (Pascal)* "Man is a thinking
reed."

8.10.2 With *"en"*

The **only** preposition used with the present participle is *"en"*
("by," "while," or "upon" doing something):

***En fermant** la porte, il a laissé son chat dehors.* By closing the
door, he left his cat outside.
*Le vieillard est mort heureux **en sachant** la vérité.* The old man
died happy, upon learning the truth.
*Elle peut chanter **en dansant.*** She can sing while dancing.

Note: The **same subject** performs both actions.

8.11 *Les verbes pronominaux*

As the name implies, pronominal verbs are always accompanied by a **pronoun** *(me, te, se, nous, vous, se)*. They are used in **reciprocal, reflexive,** and **idiomatic** constructions.

8.11.1 Reciprocal

Roméo et Juiliette s'aiment. Romeo and Juliet love each other.
Nous nous écrivons chaque mois. We write to each other every
　　month. [The first *"nous"* is subject; the second is the indirect object pronoun.]
Vous vous regardez longtemps. You look at each other for a long
　　time.
Ils se voient tous les jours. They see each other every day.

8.11.2 Reflexive

The **action of the verb** falls on the **subject:**

1. *Bette se lave.* Betty gets washed (or washes herself).
2. *Bette s'est lavée.* Betty washed herself. [The auxiliary for **every pronomial verb** in compound tenses is *être.*]
3. *Bette se lave les mains.* Betty washes her hands.
4. *Bette s'est lavé les mains.* Betty washed her hands.
5. *Bette se les est lavées.* Betty washed them.

In 1 and 3, there is no agreement.

In 2, since *être* is the auxiliary, *"lavée"* agrees with the **subject.**

In 4, there is a **direct object,** *"les mains,"* which **follows** the verb. The function of *"se"* in this case is that of an **indirect object.** ("Betty washed **'to herself'** the hands.") There is **no agreement.**

In 5, the **direct object** *"les"* now **precedes** the verb. *"Se"* is still an **indirect object.** Agreement is therefore made with *"les,"* which is **feminine plural.**

Rule: With **reflexive** verbs, follow the rule of agreement for *être* (participle agrees with the **subject**) unless there is a **direct object preceding** the verb. If so, follow the rule of *avoir* (participle agrees with **object**).

8.11.3 Common Idiomatic Use of Pronominal Verbs

To express the **passive voice** (i.e., the action falls on the subject instead of an object), the **reflexive form** is often used:

*Le français **se parle** au Canada.* French is spoken in Canada.
*Monsieur, cela **ne se fait pas** ici!* Sir, that isn't done here!
*Les journaux **se vendent** au kiosk.* Papers are sold at the kiosk.

Note: The verb agrees in number with the subject.

8.12 Two Other Past Tenses of the Indicative

Two other past tenses of the indicative are *le passé simple* and *le passé antérieur.* Both of these tenses are used in writing, rather than in conversation. (Many modern writers use the *passé composé, imparfait,* and *plus-que-parfait* instead of these tenses.)

Le passé simple (historic or literary past) describes an action finished at a well-defined moment in the past.

Formation of regular verbs: Add to the stem the following endings:

–er verbs	*–ir* verbs	*–re* verbs
je parlai	*je finis*	*je vendis*
tu parlas	*tu finis*	*tu vendis*
il parla	*il finit*	*il vendit*
nous parlâmes	*nous finîmes*	*nous vendîmes*
vous parlâtes	*vous finîtes*	*vous vendîtes*
ils parlèrent	*ils finirent*	*ils vendirent*

*Napoléon **entra** dans la salle et **prit** son épée.* Napoleon entered the room and took his sword.

*Les princes **rendirent** le terrain aux paysans.* The princes gave back the land to the peasants.

8.12.1 Some Irregular Forms of the *Passé Simple*

avoir: j'eus	*être: je fus*	*savoir: je sus*
faire: je fis	*pouvoir: je pus*	*connaître: je connus*
écrire: j'écrivis	*vouloir: je voulus*	*falloir: il fallut*
lire: je lus	*voir: je vis*	*craindre: je craignis*

8.12.2 *Le passé antérieur*

Le passé antérieur, another literary tense, is used to show action that immediately precedes the *passé simple.* (Their relationship is similar to that of the *pluperfect* and the *passé composé.*)

Formation: Use the *passé simple* of *avoir* or *être* with the *past participle:*

*Quand ils **eurent trouvé** la maison, ils **frappèrent** à la porte.* When they (had) found the house, they knocked at the door.

*Marcel **arriva** aussitôt que son père **fut parti**.* Marcel arrived right after his father left.

CHAPTER 9

The Subjunctive

The subjunctive is a **mood** that communicates emotions, wishes, desires, opinions, doubts — the subjective state of mind — of one agent acting upon another. Certain factors must be present for its use:

1. There must be **two different** subjects in **two clauses: one main, one subordinate;**
2. the subordinate clause must be introduced by *"que"*;
3. an expression of emotion, doubt, necessity, etc. must be present in the main clause.

9.1   Formation: Regular Verbs

–er verbs	*–ir* verbs	*–re* verbs
que je mange	*que je dorme*	*que je rende*
que tu manges	*que tu dormes*	*que tu rendes*
qu'il mange	*qu'il dorme*	*qu'il rende*
que nous mangions	*que nous dormions*	*que nous rendions*
que vous mangiez	*que vous dormiez*	*que vous rendiez*
qu'ils mangent	*qu'ils dorment*	*qu'ils rendent*

9.1.1 Formation: Irregular Verbs

Irregular verbs have the same endings as regular verbs, except their stems are irregular.

Some common irregular forms:
faire: que je fasse
dire: que je dise
pouvoir: que je puisse
mettre: que je mette
craindre: que je craigne
vivre: que je vive
savoir: que je sache
rire: que je rie, que nous riions
lire: que je lise
écrire: que j'écrive, que nous écrivions
prendre: que je prenne, que nous prenions, qu'ils prennent
vouloir: que je veuille, que nous voulions, qu'ils veuillent
aller: que j'aille, que nous allions, qu'ils aillent
venir: que je vienne, que nous venions, qu'ils viennent
voir: que je voie, que nous voyions, qu'ils voient
boire: que je boive, que nous buvions, qu'ils boivent
mourir: que je meure, que nous mourions, qu'ils meurent
devoir: que je doive, que nous devions, qu'ils doivent

Note:

être	*avoir*
que je sois	*que j'aie*
que nous soyons	*que nous ayons*
qu'ils soient	*qu'ils aient*

9.2 Uses of the Subjunctive in Subordinate Clauses

When using the subjunctive in subordinate clauses:

With expressions of necessity:

*Il faut que Pierre me **rende** cet argent.* Peter must give that money
    back to me. (Or) It's necessary that Peter give....
*Est-ce qu'**il est nécessaire que** tu **ailles** chez tes parents?* Do
    you have to go to your parents' house?
*Ses amis **exigent que** Diane leur **écrive** des lettres.* Her friends
    insist that Diane write them letters.

With expressions of desire or will:

*Voulez-vous que nous **venions** à midi?* Do you want us to come
    at noon?
*L'enfant **préfère que** sa mère lui **tienne** la main.* The child pre-
    fers that his mother hold his hand.
*Nous **désirons que** la paix **soit** faite au monde.* We want peace to
    be made in the world.
*Je **souhaite que** Marcel te **dise** le vérité.* I wish that Marcel would
    tell you the truth.

With expressions of emotion:

*Laurent **n'aime pas que** tu **partes** si tôt.* Larry doesn't like you to
    be leaving so soon.
*Ils **ont peur que** cette voiture **ne puisse pas** faire le voyage.*
    They're afraid that this car can't make the trip.
*Votre père **est heureux que** vous **compreniez** le problème.* Your
    father is glad that you understand the problem.

With expressions of doubt:

*Il est **douteux que** nous **fassions** ce dîner.* It's doubtful that we'll
    make that dinner.
*Je **ne suis pas certaine que** Jean **vienne** avec nous.* I'm not sure
    John's coming with us.
*Elle **n'est pas convaincue que** cette situation **soit** bonne.* She's
    not convinced that this situation is a good one.

With impersonal expressions (that convey a **subjective** idea):

Il est important que tu étudies cette leçon. It's important that you study this lesson.

Il est temps que nous nous en allions. It's time for us to leave.

C'est dommage que tu ne saches pas son adresse. It's too bad you don't know her address.

Il est inutile que vous vous dépêchiez. It's useless for you to hurry.

Il est possible que cet homme veuille travailler ici. It's possible that this man wants to work here.

Note: When there is more **certainty** than doubt, the **indicative** is used:

Il est probable que nous allons à Marseille. We will probably go to Marseilles.

Elle est certaine que son mari peut réparer la télé. She's sure her husband can repair the TV.

On est sûr que les voisins ont acheté une nouvelle maison. We're sure the neighbors bought a new house.

Sans doute que Richard gagnera plus que toi. Probably Richard will earn more than you.

With *espérer, penser,* and *croire:* When these verbs are **in the affirmative** ("I hope," "I think," "I believe"), the verb is in the **indicative:**

Vous espérez que leur avion partira à l'heure. You hope their plane will leave on time.

Je pense que Sylvie est très intelligente. I think Sylvia is very smart.

Le petit croit que son père va jouer avec lui. The child thinks his father will play with him.

However, when these verbs are either **negative** or **interrogative,** since there may be doubt involved, the **subjunctive** is used:

Je n'espère pas qu'elle m'écrive. I don't hope she'll write me.

Pense-t-il que sa cousine revienne bientôt? Does he think his cousin will be back soon?

Je ne crois pas que Sara puisse nous accompagner. I don't think Sara can go with us.

9.3 Uses of Subjunctive after Certain Conjunctions

After certain conjunctions which convey a sense of doubt or fear, the subjunctive is required:

Avant que tu le saches, l'hiver arrivera. Before you know it, winter will be here.

Pourvu que mes amis voient Robert, ils nous téléphoneront. Provided that my friends see Robert, they'll call us.

9.3.1 Conjunctions and Prepositions

Many of these conjunctions have corresponding **prepositions** which are used when there is only **one subject:**

Conjunction (+ Subjunctive) (Two subjects)	Preposition (+ Infinitive) (One subject for both actions)
à condition que – provided that	*à condition de*
afin que – in order that	*afin de*
à moins que – unless	*à moins de*
avant que – before	*avant de*
de crainte que – for fear that	*de crainte de*
de peur que – for fear that	*de peur de*
pour que – so that	*pour*

De crainte d'oublier le rendez-vous, j'ai écrit la date. For fear of forgetting the appointment, I wrote down the date.

Elle achètera cette voiture, à condition d'avoir assez d'argent. She'll buy that car, provided that she has enough money.

Avant de partir, viens nous voir. Before you leave, come see us.

9.3.2 Conjunctions with the Subjunctive

Some conjunctions do not have a prepositional equivalent and require the **subjunctive, even with one subject:**

bien que – although	*de sorte que* – so that
malgré que – despite the fact that	*pourvu que* – provided that
jusqu'à ce que – until	*quoique* – although

Bien qu'il dorme beaucoup, il est toujours fatigué. Although he sleeps a lot, he's always tired.

Elle attendra ici jusqu'à ce qu'elle apprenne le résultat. She'll wait here until she finds out the results.

Quoique Sam fasse de son mieux, il ne réussit pas. Although Sam is doing his best, he isn't succeeding.

Note: The form *"quoi que"* (two words meaning "whatever" or "no matter what") also takes the subjunctive:

Quoi que tu dises, on ne va pas te croire. No matter what you say, they won't believe you.

9.4 *Le passé du subjonctif*

The **past subjunctive** is a comparative tense used to contrast **an action in one tense** (in the principal clause) with **an action that preceded it** (in the subordinate clause). The auxiliary *avoir* or *être*, in the **subjunctive form**, is used with the **past participle.**

Nous sommes contents que nos amis soient enfin arrivés. We're happy (now) that our friends finally arrived (before now).

Est-ce que tu étais surprise que Jeanne t'ait envoyé l'argent? Were you surprised (yesterday) that Jean had sent you the money?

Maurice n'a pas cru que sa fille soit née. Maurice didn't believe his daughter had already been born.

9.4.1   Agreement of Tenses *(La concordance du temps)*

With two **simultaneous actions,** i.e., those that take place **at the same time** or in **rapid chronological order,** the **present subjunctive** is used, **even in past contexts:**

*Monique **était heureuse que** Virginie **ne parte pas.** Monica was happy that Virginia wasn't leaving.
*Il **a parlé** lentement **afin que** nous **puissions** le comprendre.* He spoke slowly so that we were able to understand him.
*Il **fallait que** les employés **fassent** attention au patron.* The employees had to pay attention to the boss.
*Je **voulais que** mes amis **suivent** l'autre route.* I wanted my friends to take the other route.
*Tout le monde **doute que** Jacques **revienne** demain.* Everyone doubts that Jack's coming back tomorrow.

CHAPTER 10

Adverbs

As in English, French adverbs modify verbs, adjectives, or other adverbs. There are adverbs of time, place, manner, quantity, negation, opinion, and adverbs that link ideas.

10.1 Formation of Adverbs

Many adverbs are formed by adding the suffix *"–ment"* (equivalent to the English suffix "–ly") to the **feminine** form of the adjective:

heureux	*heureuse*	*heureusement* (happily, luckily)
lent	*lente*	*lentement* (slowly)
doux	*douce*	*doucement* (softly, slowly, gently)
égal	*égale*	*également* (equally)
certain	*certaine*	*certainement* (certainly, surely)

10.1.1 Adjectives that End with Vowels

Adjectives that end in "e" or in **another vowel,** simply add *"–ment"*:

rapide	*rapidement*	*vrai*	*vraiment* (really, truly)
sincère	*sincèrement*	*absolu*	*absolument*
infini	*infiniment*		

10.2 Irregular Forms

(a) *Bien — mieux.*

(b) Adjectives that end in *"–ant"* and *"–ent"* form their adverbs by adding *"–amment"* or *"–emment"* as suffixes:

constant	*constamment*	*Elle chante **constamment**.* She sings constantly.
prudent	*prudemment*	*Nous avons agi **prudemment**.* We acted prudently (cautiously).
courant	*couramment*	*Parlent-ils **couramment**?* Do they speak (French) fluently?

(c) Some adjectives form adverbs with the suffix *"–ément":*

profond	*profondément*	*Nous avons été **profondément** émus.* We were deeply (profoundly) moved.
précis	*précisément*	*Vous avez reçu **précisément** ce que vous vouliez.* You received just what you wanted.
décidé	*décidément*	*C'était **décidément** sérieux.* It was decidedly (definitely) serious.
assuré	*assurément*	*Vous serez **assurément** à l'heure.* You'll surely be on time.

(d) *bref – brièvement. Il a parlé brièvement.* He spoke briefly.
(e) *gentil – gentiment. Elle m'a répondu gentiment.* She answered me politely.

10.3 Placement of the Adverb

The adverb **precedes** an **adjective** or another **adverb**:

*Sam était **complètement** surpris.* Sam was completely surprised.
*Il m'a parlé **bien** sérieusement.* He spoke to me quite seriously.

10.3.1 With Simple Verbs

The adverb **follows** a simple verb:

*Nous le lui dirons **doucement**.* We'll tell him gently.
*Yves allait **souvent** chez eux.* Yves used to go to their house often.

10.3.2 With Compound Verbs

With a **compound** verb, the adverb **follows the auxiliary** (especially with short forms) or may **follow the participle** (with forms in "*–ment*"):

*Simone est **presque** partie sans nous.* Simone nearly left without us.
*Il a **toujours** aimé jouer.* He has always loved to play.
*Elle a **déjà** fini.* She finished already.
*Nous lui avons parlé **calmement**.* We spoke to her calmly.
*Ils sont entrés **bruyamment**.* They came in noisely.

10.3.3 Adverbs of Time and Space

Place adverbs of time and space **after** the participle or at the **beginning** of the sentence:

***Hier** nous avons vu Charles.* We saw Charles yesterday.
*Le cheval est tombé **là-bas**.* The horse fell down over there.
*Vous m'avez **souvent** écrit **autrefois**.* You often wrote me in the past.

Note: *Souvent* (often), *déjà* (already), and *toujours* (always) are placed **before** the participle.

10.4   Comparative of Adverbs

As with adjectives, add *"aussi," "plus"* or *"moins"* for equal, superior, or inferior comparisons:

> *Nous avons voyagé **aussi longtemps** qu'eux.* We traveled as long as they did.
> *Jean écrit **plus correctement** que toi.* John writes more correctly than you.
> *Sara nous parlait **moins librement** que Bette.* Sara spoke to us less freely than Betty did.

Hint: Remember that the comparative of *"bien"* is *"mieux"* (better) **without** *"plus."* For **"less well,"** use *"moins bien":*

> *Angélique parle allemand **moins bien** que sa soeur.* Angelique speaks German worse than her sister.
> *Sophie chante **mieux** que moi.* Sophie sings better than I do.

10.5   The Superlative

The superlative is formed by adding *"le"* to the comparative form and is **invariable:**

> *Nancy danse **le plus gracieusement** de toute la famille.* Nancy dances the most gracefully of everyone in the family.
> *C'est Philippe qui téléphone **le moins souvent**.* Phillip's the one who phones the least often.

10.6   Some Common Adverbs

Of quantity:

assez – enough	*très* – very
trop – too, too much	*tant* – so much
peu – little	

Of manner:

haut – high, loud	*bas* – low, quietly
vite – quickly	

Of time:

    toujours – always, still   *jamais* – never

    hier – yesterday   *aujourd'hui* – today

    demain – tomorrow   *autrefois* – in the past

Of place:

    ici – here   *là, là-bas* – there

    dehors – outside   *loin* – far

Of assent, dissent and reasoning:

    pourquoi – why, because   *ainsi* – thus

    néanmoins – nevertheless   *pourtant* – however

    cependant – however   *oui, non, peut-être* –

                                 yes, no, perhaps

Note: *"peut-être"* is followed by *"que"* when it begins a sentence:

Peut-être que *nous te verrons ce soir.* Perhaps we'll see you this evening.

10.7 Interrogative Adverbs

    où – where   *quand* – when

    comment – how   *pourquoi* – why

    combien – how much, how many

10.8 Adverbs that Connect Nouns, Phrases, and Clauses

    d'abord – first, at first   *ensuite* – next, then

    enfin – finally, at last   *car, parce que* – because

    mais – but

D'abord *il ouvre la porte et* **ensuite** *il appelle son chien.* First he opens the door and then he calls his dog.

CHAPTER 11

Prepositions and Conjunctions

11.1 Prepositions

A preposition introduces a phrase and has a noun, pronoun, or infinitive as its **object.** Prepositions are invariable.

Simple Prepositions:

avec – with	*sans* – without	*dans* – in
sur – on	*pour* – for	*par* – by
sous – under	*de* – of, from	*devant* – in front of
dans – in	*à* – at, to	*derrière* – behind
en – in	*contre* – against	*entre* – between

avant – before (in time)

parmi – among (more than two things). *C'est **parmi** mes papiers.* It's among my papers.

après – after (in time and space). *Viens **après** cinq hueres.* Come after 5 o'clock. *Il est arrivé après moi.* He arrived after me.

11.2 Compound Prepositions

Compound prepositions are composed of more than one word:

94

à côté de – next to	*autour de* – around (in space)
près de – near	*loin de* – far from
au-dessous de – underneath	*le long de* – along
en haut de – at the top of	*en bas de* – below
en face de – opposite	*à droite de* – to the right of
à gauche de – to the left of	*au-dessus de* – above
au milieu de – in the middle of	*jusqu'à* – until (in time and space)

11.3   Prepositions with Geographic Names

For **cities,** always use *"à"*:

Je vais à Nice. I'm going to Nice.
Ils habitent à Chicago. They live in Chicago.
Allez-vous à Rome? Are you going to Rome?
Nous arriverons à Quebec. We'll arrive in Quebec.

Note: A few cities have an **article** in their name:

On s'arrête au Havre et à la Nouvelle Orléans. We're stopping at Le Havre and New Orleans.

For **large islands,** use *"à"*:

Ils sont à Hawaii. Elles sont à Cuba. They are in Hawaii. They are in Cuba.

For **"feminine" states, provinces, countries** or **continents** (those that end in an *"e"*) use *"en"*:

Ils ont habité en Californie, en Floride, en France, en Allemagne, en Espagne, en Angleterre, en Afrique, en Europe, en Asie, en Italie, en Bretagne, et en Provence.

For **"masculine" countries** (those not ending in *"e"*) use *"au"*:

Je vais au Japon, au Portugal, au Canada, au Pérou.

Je reviens du Danemark, du Congo, du Brésil, du Maroc, des États-Unis.

Exceptions: *au Mexique; en Israël*

For the **names of states in the U.S.,** the same rule applies:

Nous voyageons en Californie, en Pennsylvanie, en Floride, et en Virginie.
Nous voyageons au Texas, au Missouri, au New Jersey, au Washington, et au Kansas.

Note: A good "rule of thumb" is to use ***"dans l'état de…"*** + **the name of the state** when you're not sure of its gender:

Il pleut beaucoup dans l'état de Nebraska, de Michigan, d'Indiana, de North Dakota, etc.

11.4 Common Verbs + Preposition + Infinitive

11.4.1 Verb + *à*

J'aide ma mère à faire le dîner. I help my mother make dinner.
Elle a commencé à danser. She started to dance.
Nous hésitons à le dire. We hesitate to say it.
On invite le professeur à parler. We invite the professor to speak.
Il s'est mis à pleurer. He started to cry.
Ont-elles réussi à finir le travail? Did they succeed in completing the work?

11.4.2 Verb + *de*

Margot accepte de lui téléphoner. Margot agrees to call him.
Simon a choisi d'acheter cette maison. Simon chose to buy this house.
Je te conseille d'aller. I advise you to go.
Continues-tu de souffrir? Are you still suffering?

Note: *Continuer* takes either *à* or *de.*

Ils ont décidé de partir. They decided to leave.
J'ai demandé à Anne de m'écrire. I asked Anne to write to me.
Il m'empêche de parler. He prevents me from speaking.

Note: See Chapter 12 for discussion of the verb *manquer.*

11.5 Conjunctions

Conjunctions join words, phrases, or clauses. **Compound conjunctions** are followed by a clause.

Commonly used **simple conjunctions** include:

et – and	*mais* – but	*ou* – or
car – because	*donc* – thus, so	*comme* – as, since
quand – when	*lorsque* – when	*or* – well, so

Commonly used **compound conjunctions** include:

parce que – because	*dès que* – as soon as
alors que – while	*puisque* – since

CHAPTER 12

Basic Idiomatic Expressions

An "idiom" cannot be translated literally.

12.1 Expressions with *avoir*

Expression	Example
avoir besoin de	*J'ai besoin d'argent.* I need money.
avoir crainte de	*Il a crainte de toi.* He's afraid of you.
avoir peur de	*Elle a peur de Jean.* She's afraid of John.
avoir honte de	*Ils ont honte de cela.* They're ashamed of it.
avoir envie de	*Tu as envie de rire.* You feel like laughing.
avoir l'air + adj.	*Elle a l'air riche.* She seems to be rich.
avoir l'air de + nom.	*Jim a l'air d'un idiot.* Jim looks like a fool.
avoir l'air de + inf.	*Il a l'air de souffrir.* He seems to be suffering.
avoir lieu	*Le concert a eu lieu hier soir.* The concert took place last night.
avoir mal	*Elle a mal à la tête.* She has a headache.
avoir chaud	*Avez-vous chaud?* Are you warm?
avoir faim	*C'est midi; j'ai faim.* It's noon; I'm hungry.
avoir soif	*Bill a toujours soif.* Bill's always thirsty.
avoir froid	*Nous avons très froid.* We're very cold.
avoir raison	*Sa mère a raison.* Her mother is right.
avoir sommeil	*As-tu sommeil?* Are you sleepy?

Expression	Example
avoir tort	*Ils **ont eu tort.*** They were wrong.
avoir + ans = age	*Claire **a 22 ans.*** Claire is 22.
avoir + âge	*Quel âge **avez**-vous?* How old are you?
avoir beau	*Tu **as beau** insister.* It's no use insisting.
avoir à + inf.	*Nous **avons à le faire.*** We have to do it.
avoir du mal + inf.	*Il **a du mal** à lire.* He has trouble reading.
en avoir à quelqu'un	*J'**en ai à Thomas.*** I've got it in for Thomas.
en avoir assez	*Sa femme **en a assez.*** His wife is fed up.
en avoir pour + time	*J'**en ai pour une heure.*** It will take me an hour.
il y a	***Il y a** six livres ici.* There are six books here.
il y a + time	*Je l'ai vu **il y a un mois.*** I saw him a month ago.
	***Il y a un an** que je l'ai vu.* It's a year since I saw him.
il n'y a pas de quoi	*Merci, madame. **Il n'y a pas de quoi.*** Thanks, madam. Don't mention it. [Often: ***"Pas de quoi."***]

12.2 Expressions with *faire*

ça, cela fait + time:

***Cela fait un an** que tu étudies.* You've been studying for a year.

Expression	Example
ça fait	*Arrête! **Ça fait** mal!* Stop! That hurts!
	***Ça** te **fera** du bien.* It will do you good.
faire semblant de	*Il **fait semblant de** l'aimer.* He pretends to like it.
s'en faire	*Ne vous **en faites** pas!* Don't worry!
faire la connaissance	*Enchanté de **faire votre connaissance.*** I'm pleased to meet you.

Expression	Example
faire un voyage	*Ils font beaucoup de voyages.* They travel a lot.
faire une promenade	*Faites une promenade.* Go for a walk.
faire le plein	*Je fais toujours le plein.* I always fill the gas tank.
faire de la fièvre	*Le bébé a fait de la fièvre.* The baby had a fever.
faire Paris-Nîmes	*Le TGV fait Paris-Nîmes en trois heures.* The TGV goes from Paris to Nimes in three hours.
faire les magasins	*Anne faisait tous les magasins.* Anne went to all the stores.
faire un rôle	*Il va faire Roméo.* He's going to play Romeo.
n'avoir que faire de	*Je n'ai que faire de tes promesses!* I don't need your promises!
faire attention	*Fais attention!* Watch out! [Pay attention!]
faire face à quelque chose	*Irène fait face à tous ses problèmes.* Irene is dealing with all her problems.
faire partie de	*Ils font partie du club.* They belong to the club.
faire de son mieux	*As-tu fait de ton mieux à l'examen?* Did you do your best on the exam?
faire sa médecine	*Simone fait sa médecine à Nice.* Simone is studying medicine in Nice.
faire ses valises	*Faites vos valises!* Pack your bags!
se faire à quelque chose	*Nous nous faisons à la situation.* We're getting used to the situation.

12.2.1 *Faire causatif*

The **subject causes someone else to do the action:**

Il se fait construire une maison. He's having a house built for himself.

Elle se fait toujours remarquer. She always makes people notice her.

Nous ferons jouer cette musique. We'll have that music played.

Il s'est fait faire un complet. He had a suit made for himself.

Ils ont fait lire l'histoire par l'enfant. They had the child read the story.

12.3 Impersonal Expressions with *il*

Time:

Il est deux heures; il est minuit; il est trois heures moins le quart. [See Chapter 3 for a discussion of time.]

Il fait jour. It's daybreak.

Il fait nuit. Night is falling.

Il se fait tard. It's getting late.

Weather:

Il fait beau; mauvais; froid; chaud; lourd; frais. It's a beautiful day; nasty; cold; hot; humid; cool.

Il fait du soleil; des nuages; de la pluie; du brouillard. It's sunny; cloudy; rainy; foggy.

12.3.1 Other Idiomatic Expressions with *il*

Il s'agit de: it's a question of; it's a matter of; it deals with

Dans ce film, il s'agit de justice. This film is about (concerns itself with) justice.

Note: The verb *"s'agir"* is **only** conjugated in the third person masculine singular (like *falloir* = *il faut*).

Il s'agit de is usually prefaced by *"Dans ce livre/roman/film/..."* or *"Dans cette situation..."* The past tense is expressed by the imperfect form of *il s'agissait de..."* (It was a question of...; a matter of...)

il arrive	*Il arrive que Georges est malade.* It happens that George is sick.
il reste	*Il nous reste dix francs.* We have 20 francs left.
il vaut [mieux]	*Il vaut mieux lui écrire.* It's better to write him.
il convient	*Il convient de téléphoner.* It's proper to phone.
il suffit de	*Il suffit de m'emvoyer une carte postale.* It's enough if you send me a post card.
il importe de	*Il importe d'arriver à temps.* It's important to arrive on time.

12.3.2 To Make General Observations

Use the formula *il est* + **adjective** + *de* + **infinitive:**

Il est important de bien manger. It's important to eat well.
Est-il nécessaire de le lui dire? Is it necessary to tell it to him?
Il est triste de ne pas la voir. It's sad not to see her.
Il est possible d'être content. It's possible to be happy.

12.3.3 *Il faut que* + subjunctive

Il faut que je parte maintenant. I must leave now.
Il ne faut pas que vos amis sachent la vérité. Your friends must not know the truth.
Faut-il que nous venions à midi? Do we have to come at noon?

To **avoid the subjunctive** with *"il faut,"* use an **indirect object pronoun** + **the infinitive:**

Il ne lui fallait pas rester. She didn't have to stay.
Est-ce qu'il leur faut déménager? Must they move?
Il nous faudra passer chez eux. We'll have to go by their house.
Vous a-t-il fallu travailler? Did you have to work?

12.4 Idiomatic Expressions with *être*

être sur le champ de faire quelque chose	*Elle **est sur le champ de se marier.*** She's about to get married.
être d'accord	***Es-tu d'accord** avec moi?* Do you agree with me?
être en train de	*Nous **sommes en train de** dîner.* We're in the midst of having dinner.
être plus fort	*C'est **plus fort** que moi!* It's too much for me.
être d'avis de	*Papa **est** toujours **de ton avis.*** Dad always agrees with you.
être de retour	*Le chef **sera de retour** demain.* The boss will be back tomorrow.
être dans son assiette	*Il n'est pas **dans son assiette.*** He doesn't feel very well.
être bien	***Etes-vous bien** dans ce lit?* Are you comfortable in that bed?
en être	*Nous **en sommes** à la page 29.* We're up to page 29.
y être	*J'**y suis.*** I've got it! (to understand, to "get it")

12.5 The Verb *manquer*

Manquer: to miss, to fail, to be short of, "nearly"

***J'ai manqué** le train.* I missed the train.
*Ne **manquez pas** de nous avertir.* Don't fail to let us know.
*As-tu tout l'argent necessaire? --Non, **il me manque** cinq francs.* Do you have all the money you need? --No, I'm five francs short.
*Elise **a manqué de** tomber.* Elise nearly fell.

Note: "Missing someone" is expressed by "He/she **is missing to me**" rather than by "I miss him/her":

*Pierre est parti; **il nous manque.*** Pierre left; we miss him.

*Où est Agnes? Elle **me manque.*** Where's Agnes? I miss her.
*Puisque leur mère habitait très loin, **elle leur manquait.*** Since
their mother lived very far away, they missed her.
*Quand tu seras en vacances sans Anne, **tu lui manqueras.*** When
you're on vacation without Anne, she'll miss you.

12.6 Measuring Time with *depuis/depuis que*

To express the passage of time from one point in the past to another point, either in the past alone or including the present, use ***depuis***
+ measure of time:

*Marc **étudie** le piano **depuis deux ans.*** Mark has been studying
the piano for two years. [The verb is in the **present** because
he's still studying.]

*François **travaillait** à Boston **depuis six mois quand** il a rencontré
Monique.* Francis had been working in Boston for six months
when he met Monique. [The verbs are in the imperfect and
passé composé because both actions are in the past and do
not extend to the present.]

12.6.1 Using *depuis que* with a Subject and Verb

***Depuis que tu as rencontré** Cécile, tu sors plus souvent.* Since
you met Cecelia, you go out more often.
*Nous sommes moins nerveux **depuis que nous avons** un chien.*
We've been less nervous since we have a dog.
*Il ne nous voit plus jamais **depuis qu'il s'est blessé.*** He never
sees us anymore since he was hurt.

Note: Don't confuse *depuis* (since) with *pendant* (during or
while):

*Il a plu **pendant** la nuit.* It rained during the night.
*Nous travaillons **pendant** l'été.* We work during the summer.

Use *pendant que* with a **subject and verb**:

Pendant que Maurice parlait, tout le monde s'endormait. Everyone fell asleep while Maurice was talking.
Pendant que j'y pense, prenez la clé. While I'm thinking of it, take the key.

12.7 *Connaître* and *savoir*

While both verbs may be translated as "to know," French differentiates between knowing people, places, works of art (including wine!), i.e., what one learns primarily through the senses, and things that one learns intellectually, by studying, practicing or learning.

*Mon frère **connaît** bien **Rome et Paris** mais je **connais mieux New York et Los Angeles**.* My brother knows Rome and Paris well but I know New York and Los Angeles better.
Connaissez-vous les Duval? Savez-vous leur adresse? Do you know the Duvals? Do you know their address?
*Jeanne **connaît un bon restaurant** où l'**on sait préparer** une bouillabaisse formidable.* Jean knows a good restaurant where they know how to make a great fish stew.
Savent-ils que ta voiture est en panne? Connaissent-ils un garagiste honnête? Do they know that your car broke down? Are they acquainted with an honest mechanic?
*Elle **connaît la musique** de Chopin et elle **sait la jouer** aussi.* She knows Chopin's music and how to play it, too.

12.8 Miscellaneous Expressions

vouloir dire:
*Que **veut dire** "ordinateur?"* What does *"ordinateur"* mean?

se rendre compte:
*Il **se rend compte** de sa faute.* He realizes his mistake.

tout de suite:
*Venez **tout de suite**!* Come at once!

rendre visite à quelqu'un:
Je rendrai visite à ma tante ce weekend. I'll visit my aunt this weekend.

Note: *Voir* or *rendre visite* are used for visiting **a person.** *Visiter* is used for **a place:** *Vas-tu visiter Chicago?*

n'en pouvoir plus:
Le pauvre chaton n'en peut plus. The poor kitten is exhausted.

passer un examen:
A-t-elle passé l'examen? Did she take the test?

réussir un examen:
Oui, et elle l'a réussi. Yes, and she passed it.

passer une nuit blanche:
Je suis très fatiguée; j'ai passé une nuit blanche. I'm very tired; I spent a sleepless night.

à la fois:
Ils sont à la fois gentils et bêtes. They're both nice and foolish at the same time.

en même temps:
Nous sommes arrivés en même temps que Julie. We arrived at the same time as Julie.

à son gré:
Le dîner était à notre gré. The dinner was to our liking.

CHAPTER 13

Negation

There are always **two** parts to a negative expression: *ne* precedes the verb and another expression follows it *(pas, jamais, aucun, etc.)*.

13.1 Positive and Negative Adverbial Expressions

encore: still	*Fabian chante-t-il encore?* Does Fabian still sing?
ne...plus	*Non, il ne chante plus.* He no longer sings.
toujours: always	*Irène sort-elle toujours avec ces jeunes gens?* Does Irene always go out with those young people?
ne...jamais	*Elle ne sort jamais avec eux.* She never goes out with them.
partout: everywhere	*Va-t-elle partout ce soir?* Is she going everywhere tonight?
ne...nulle part	*Elle ne va nulle part.* She's not going anywhere.
déjà: already	*Ont-ils déjà déjeuné?* Have they already had lunch?
ne...pas encore	*Non, ils ne sont pas encore descendus.* No, they haven't come down yet.

et: both, and	*Nous avons rencontré et Claude et David. Ont-ils téléphoné?* We met Claude and David. Did they call?
ni...ni...ne	*Ni Claude ni David n'ont téléphoné.* Neither Claude nor David has phoned.

Note: The verb is **plural** in French for **"neither, nor."**

13.1.1 Other Negations

ne...pas	*Tu n'as pas d'amis ici.* You have no friends here.
ne...guère	*Elle n'a guère répondu.* She hardly answered.
ne...que	*Elise n'a que deux chapeaux.* Elise has only two hats.
ne...aucun	*Il n'a lu aucun livre cet été.* He hasn't read a single book this summer.

Note: *"Aucun"* can be used as a **pronoun** as well as an **adjective.** The verb is always in the **singular:**

A-t-elle reçu mes lettres? --Non, aucune n'est arrivée. Did she receive my letters? No, not one has arrived.

ne...personne	*Personne ne nous a téléphoné.* No one called us.
ne...rien	*Rien n'est important quand on est malade.* Nothing is important when you're sick.
ne...ni...ni	*Charles ne veut ni écouter ni discuter l'histoire.* Charles neither wants to listen to the story nor to discuss it.

13.2 *Quelque chose de/rien de* + Adjective

To express the general idea of "something" or "nothing" + an adjective, use *quelque chose de* or *rien de:*

Patrice, as-tu quelque chose d'intéressant à nous raconter? Non,
je n'ai rien d'important à vous dire. Patricia, do you have
something interesting to tell us? No, I've nothing of importance to say to you.

Est-ce que quelque chose d'amusant est arrivé? Rien d'amusant
n'est arrivé. Did something amusing happen? Nothing amusing took place.

Avez-vous acheté quelque chose de délicieux au marché? Non,
il n'y avait rien de délicieux à acheter. Did you buy something delicious in the market? No, there was nothing delicious to buy.

Note: The adjective is always masculine singular in these structures.

For "someone," "anyone," or "nobody" use *"quelqu'un de"* or
"personne de":

Connaissent-ils quelqu'un de riche et de célèbre? Non, ils ne
connaissent personne de riche ni de célèbre. Do they know
anyone rich and famous? No, they don't know anybody who's
rich and famous.

Est-ce que quelqu'un d'intelligent ferait cela? Non, personne
d'intelligent ne le ferait. Would someone intelligent do that?
No, nobody intelligent would do it.

CHAPTER 14

Useful Vocabulary

14.1   School (*L'école*)

s'inscrire aux cours – to register for classes
assister au cours – to attend class
l'école élémentaire – grammar school
le lycée – high school

l'horaire – schedule
échouer, rater – to fail

la biblio(thèque) – the library
des livres d'occasion – used books
sa spécialité – one's major

l'assistance – attendance

un mémoire – a paper
le collège – middle school

prendre son diplôme – to graduate
réussir – to pass
des cours obligatoires – required classes
la librairie – the bookstore
l'ordinateur – computer

14.2   Animals (*Un animal; Les animaux*)

le boeuf – bull
le cerf – deer
le coq – rooster
le mouton – sheep
le chien – dog

la vache – cow
la biche – doe
la poule – hen
le chat – tomcat

un(e) mulet – mule (both masculine and feminine)
un âne – donkey
un poisson – a fish
un ours – bear

un cheval – horse
un lapin – rabbit
un renard – fox
un oiseau – bird

14.3 The Body (*Le corps*)

la tête – head

les oreilles – ears (fem.)
la chevelure – head of hair
les lèvres – lips
la langue – tongue
la poitrine – chest
la jambe – leg
le pied – foot
le bras – arm
le poignet – wrist
le dos – the back
le coeur – heart

un oeil; les yeux – one eye, the eyes
les cheveux – hair
la bouche – mouth
les dents – teeth (fem.)
le cou – neck
le ventre – stomach
le genou – knee
la cheville – ankle
le coude – elbow
la main – hand
l'épaule – shoulder (fem.)
le foie – liver

14.4 The City (*La ville*)

le centre ville – downtown
visiter la ville – sightseeing in town
la visite – a tour
Où se trouve...? – Where is...?
à gauche – to the left
la place – the square
la rue – the street
le boulevard – boulevard
le musée – museum
le parc – the park
la banque – the bank

la préfecture – police station

la cité – old part of town
une excursion – guided sightseeing tour
l'hôtel de ville – town hall
à la droite – to the right
tout droit – straight ahead
la fontaine – fountain
le trottoir – the sidewalk
le cinéma – the movies
tarif, droit d'entrée – admission fee
un banc – a bench
les chèques de voyage – travelers checks
l'agent de police – policeman

le bureau de poste – post office   des timbres – stamps
le jardin zoologique – the zoo   l'agence de voyage – travel agency
Renseignements – Information (booth)

14.5   Clothing *(Les vêtements)*

un chemisier – a blouse   une jupe – a skirt
un pantalon – pants   un chapeau – a hat
un sac – a purse   une robe – a dress
les chaussures – shoes   un tailleur – a suit
un maillot – a bathing suit   les gants – gloves
la veste – a jacket (suit)   un blouson – outside jacket
un manteau – a coat   l'écharpe – scarf
des bas – stockings   le short – shorts
une robe de chambre – bathrobe   le bleu-jean – jeans
l'imperméable (l'imper) –   le tricot, le pull, le chandail –
     a raincoat   sweater, pullover
les chaussettes – socks   une ceinture – belt
un complet – suit   une chemise – a shirt
une cravate – a tie   un gilet – a vest

14.6   Colors *(Les couleurs)*

le bleu – blue   le jaune – yellow
le gris – gray   le blanc – white
le noir – black   le rouge – red
le rose – pink   le vert – green
le pourpre – purple   le brun – brown
le beige – beige   le marron – chestnut brown

14.7   Drinks *(Les boissons)*

le vin – wine   un demi – glass of beer
la bière – beer   le jus de fruits – fruit juice
l'eau minérale – mineral water   la limonade – soda (7-Up)
le citronnade – lemonade   le soda – soda
le coca – Coke   le sucre – sugar
la boisson gazeuse – soft drink le café – coffee

le café crème – coffee with cream

le café au lait – coffee with milk cream

le café nature – black coffee

le café turc – Turkish coffee

le café express – espresso coffee

le lait – milk

le café décaféiné – decaffeinated coffee

une demi-tasse – small cup of coffee, black, very strong

le thé – tea

le thé anglais – tea with milk

le thé glacé – iced tea

un apéritif (l'apéro) – cocktail

le chocolat chaud – hot chocolate

un digestif – a liqueur; after-dinner drink

14.8   The Family (*La famille*)

le père – the father

la mère – the mother

un bébé – a baby

un(e) enfant – child (boy or girl)

un garçon – boy

une fille – girl, daughter

le fils – son

papa, maman – dad, mom

la tante – aunt

l'oncle – uncle

la grand-mère – grandmother

le grand-père – grandfather

le cousin, la cousine – cousin

le neveu – nephew

la nièce – niece

14.9   Foods (*Les aliments*)

Fruits (*Les fruits*):

une banane – banana

une pomme – apple

une poire – pear

une pêche – peach

une prune – plum

une orange – orange

une cerise – cherry

un abricot – apricot

une fraise – strawberry

une framboise – raspberry

un ananas – pineapple

un citron – lemon

un pamplemousse – grapefruit

du raisin sec – raisins

Vegetables (*Les légumes*):

une carotte – carrot

une tomate – tomato

une pomme de terre – potato

une laitue – lettuce

un oignon – onion

un haricot – bean

le maïs – corn les petits pois – peas
le brocoli – broccoli les épinards – spinach
le poivron – pepper le concombre – cucumber
    (red or green)

Meat and Poultry (*La viande et la volaille*):

le boeuf – beef le bifteck – steak
le veau – veal le jambon – ham
le porc – pork les saucisses – sausage
le mouton – lamb le poulet – chicken
le canard – duck la dinde – turkey

Desserts (*Les desserts*):

la tarte aux pommes – apple pie la tarte aux fruits – fruit pie
la glace – ice cream les parfums – flavors
la crème brûlée – custard un petit gâteau – cookie
un beignet – doughnut le gaufre – waffle
une crêpe – thin pancake le yaourt – yogurt
la pâtisserie – pastry le chou à la crème – cream puff
le gâteau au chocolat –
    chocolate cake

14.10 Illnesses (*Les maladies*)

avoir mal... – to have pain in…

aller chez le médecin – to go to être allergique – to be allergic
    the doctor's office
avoir les frissons – to have chills la douleur – pain
la tension – blood pressure le pouls – pulse
avoir des nausées – to be vomir – to throw up
    nauseous
l'antibiotique – antibiotic le médicament – medicine
la pîqure – an injection une pilule – a pill
démangeaison – an itching une éruption – a rash
un rhume – a cold la grippe – the flu
l'hôpital – hospital l'infirmière – the nurse
l'ordonnance – prescription l'honoraire – doctor's fee

14.11 Professions, Occupations *(Les professions, les métiers)*

Note: For many professions, there is no female form. The word *"femme"* or *"une"* precedes the profession or the masculine form is used.

un(e) avocat(e) – lawyer
un ingénieur – engineer
un, une secrétaire – secretary
une actrice – actress
un chauffeur de taxi –
    taxi driver
un serveur, une serveuse –
    waiter, waitress
un commis – clerk

la ménagère – housewife

le fermier, la fermière – farmer
le pharmacien, la pharma-
    cienne – pharmacist
un pilote – pilot

un juge – judge
un chef – cook
un acteur – actor
un, une artiste – artist
un professeur – secondary or
    college teacher
un vendeur, une venduese –
    salesperson
le coiffeur, la coiffeuse –
    hairdresser
le policier, la policière –
    policeman, policewoman
le banquier – banker
un chimiste – chemist

un musicien, une musicienne –
    musician

Glossary

aïeul; aïeux (m.) – ancestor; ancestors
aile (m.) – wing
à la carte – from the menu (singly chosen items)
Allemagne (f.) – Germany
allemand(e) (adj.) – German
américain(e) (adj.) – American
Américain(e) – American person
animé(e) – lively; busy
au pair (m.) – a person who works for room and board

berger (m.) – shepherd
beurre (m.) – butter
boeuf (m.) – beef; ox; steer
boire – to drink
boisson (f.) – a drink
bonheur (m.) – happiness
bonté (f.) – kindness
bout (m.) – end; bottom
breton (adj.) – Breton (from Brittany)
bureau (m.) – desk; office

cadet (m.) – younger of two children; youngest
caisse (f.) – cash register (where you pay a bill)
campagne (f.) – countryside
chaîne (f.) – TV channel
chef-d'oeuvre (m.) – masterpiece
chèque (m.) – check (bank)
chez – at the house of
chiffon (m.) – rag
choisir – to choose
chronique (f.) – chronical; newspaper column

clé; clef (f.) – key
coiffeuse (f.) – hairdresser; dressing table
commencer – to begin
compter – to count
concours (m.) – contest
connaître – to know; be acquainted with
conseiller – to advise
cou (m.) – neck
coup d'état (m.) – sudden overthrow of a government
coup de grâce (m.) – death blow
craindre – to fear
croire – to believe

debout (adv., adj.; invariable) – standing
déception (f.) – disappointment
déçu (adj.) – disappointed
de luxe – luxurious
demain (m.) – tomorrow
demander – to ask
détente – easing of political tensions
dette (f.) – debt
deuil (m.) – mourning
devoir– to have to do something; (noun; m.) duty
dire – to say; tell

eau (f.) – water
écrire – to write
empêcher – to prevent; impede
emporter – to carry off; take something along
enfant (m., f.) – child
enseigner – to teach
entendre – to hear; understand
envoyer – to send
essayer – to try
éteindre – to extinguish; shut off
étendre – to stretch

faire – to make; to do
fait accompli (m.) – accomplished fact; a "done deed"
faveur (f.) – favor
fête (f.) – party; festival; feast
fontaine (f.) – fountain
force de frappe (f.) – striking force (army)
français (adj., m.) – French (language or thing)
Français(e) (m., f.) – Frenchman; Frenchwoman

garçon – boy; waiter
gare (f.) – railway station
gêne (f.) – embarrassment; discomfort; trouble
gilet (m.) – vest; cardigan
gourmand (m.) – a big eater
gourmet (m.) – a discriminating eater
grand prix (m.) – first prize
guêpe (f.) – wasp
guérir – to cure; heal
guerre (f.) – war

habiter – to live (in a place); reside
haïr – to hate
haut; haute – high; loud
hier (m.) – yesterday

imiter – to imitate
inégal(e) – unequal
irréel (f.) – unreal

jaune – yellow
jeune – young

klaxon (m.) – car horn

liaison (f.) – a relationship; linking of consonant and vowel
lisse (adj.) – smooth; sleek

mal (m.) – evil; pain; (adverb) badly
mèche (f.) – lock of hair; wick
médecin (m.) – doctor
médecine – medicine
médicament – medication
même – same; self; very same
menace (f.) – a threat
mener – to lead someone
merveille (f.) – marvel
mois (m.) – month
mot-clef (m.) – key word
moulin (m.) – mill

naissance (f.) – birth
naître – to be born
négation (f.)   negative forms, negation
neige (f.) – snow
nom (m.) – name; noun
nuage (m.) – cloud

oeil; yeux (m.) – eye; eyes
oeuf (m.) – egg
ôter – to remove; lift; take away
ou – or
où – where
ouest (m.) – west
ouïr – to hear

paix (f.) – peace
palais (m.) – palace; palate
pareil; pareille – similar; the same
peine (f.) – sorrow; sadness; effort
plaisir (m.) – pleasure
profond (adj.) – deep; profound

quai (m.) – dock; wharf

raconter – to recount; tell a story
rencontrer – to meet; encounter someone
rester – to stay; remain
rhume (m.) – a cold
rire – to laugh

sale (adj.) – dirty
salle (f.) – room
sauce (f.) – gravy; salad dressing; sauce
savoir – to know
sec (adj., m.) – dry
sécheresse (f.) – drought
sel (m.) – salt
soif (f.) – thirst
soir (m.) – evening
sortie (f.) – exit; military action
souffrir – to suffer
soulier (m.) – shoe

tête (f.) – head
tirade (f.) – long speech in a play; tirade
tôt – early
travail (m.) – work
travailler – to work
trompe-l'oeil (m.) – style of art that appears to be something it isn't
trou (m.) – hole
trouver – to find

usine (f.) – factory
utile – useful

vérité (f.) – truth
vif (adj.) – lively; bright (color)
vilain (adj.) – ugly; nasty; wicked
visiter – to see (a place, not a person); to tour
voir – to see

wagon (m.) – railway car